Surveillance after September 11

Titles in this series

Surveillance after September 11

DAVID LYON

polity

The right of David Lyon to be identified as Author of this Work has been asserted in accordance with the UK Copyright, Designs and Patents Act 1988.

First published in 2003 by Polity Press in association with Blackwell Publishing Ltd.

Editorial office:
Polity Press
65 Bridge Street
Cambridge CB2 1UR, UK

Marketing and production:
Blackwell Publishing Ltd
108 Cowley Road
Oxford OX4 1JF, UK

Distributed in the USA by
Blackwell Publishing Inc.
350 Main Street
Malden, MA 02148, USA

ISBN: 0–7456 3180–0
ISBN: 0–7456 3181–9 (pb)

A catalogue record for this book is available from the British Library.

Library of Congress Cataloging-in-Publication Data
Lyon, David, 1948-
Surveillance after September 11 / David Lyon.
    p. cm. – (Themes for the 21st century)
Includes bibliographical references and index.
ISBN 0–7456–3180–0 ISBN 0–7456 3181–9 (pb)
1. Social control—United States. 2. Social control—Political aspects—United States.
3. Electronic surveillance—Social aspects—United States. 4. Political culture—United States. 5. Privacy, Right of—United States. 6. War on Terrorism, 2001– I. Title.
II. Series.
HN59.2 .L96 2003
303.3'3—dc21
        2003001340

Typeset in 10.5 on 12 Plantin
by SetSystems Ltd, Saffron Walden, Essex
Printed and bound in Great Britain by
TJ International, Padstow, Cornwall

For further information on Polity, visit our website: www.polity.co.uk

Contents

Preface and Acknowledgments

Thanks are due to friends and colleagues in the Surveillance Project at Queen's University and to others, in Canada and elsewhere, who have kindly commented on earlier drafts of this book. They are Perri 6 Ian Barns, Colin Bennett, Bart Bonikowski, Craig Calhoun, Yolande Chan, Richard Day, Lynsey Dubbeld, Gerry Gill, Sean Hier, abi lyon, Christian Leuprecht, Bill Moore, Cornelia Moser, Gina Patterson, Mark Salter, Geoff Smith, Catherine Stoehr, Irwin Streight, Donald Stuart, Ali Zaidi, Elia Zureik, two anonymous reviewers, and my editor at Polity Press, John Thompson. Thanks, too, to my research assistant, Emily Merz, and to abi lyon, who made the index. An earlier version of some ideas appeared in *Sociological Research Online*, November 2001; www.socresonline.org.uk/6/3/lyon; a somewhat different version of chapter 2 will appear in *The International Journal of Urban and Regional Research*, 2003; parts of chapter 4 were given as a paper at a conference at the Technology Assessment Institute of the Austrian Academy of Sciences in Vienna, November 11, 2002; and sections of chapter 5 appear in "Airports as Data Filters: Converging Surveillance Systems after September 11th" *Information, Communication, and Ethics in Society*, 1 (1), 2003, 13–20.

Family members also offered encouragement and comment, as well as more support than anyone could hope for, so thanks once more to Sue, Tim, abi, Josh, and Miriam.

Introduction

If you have nothing to hide, it is often said, you have nothing to fear. This was a false assumption before September 11, 2001, and its falsity has become even more palpable and pernicious since. In the "war against terrorism" the net of suspicion is being cast far and wide and no one, however remote from "terrorism," can safely imagine that they are exempt from scrutiny. The loss of some liberties is portrayed as the price paid for security, which is another dubious deal. While tracking down the perpetrators of violence is entirely appropriate and laudable, reinforcing surveillance without clear and democratically defined limits is not.

Of course, the practice of watching others in order to detect inappropriate behavior or to avert danger and risk is nothing new. Think of the biblical book of beginnings, Genesis. "Where are you?" called the Creator to the primal couple, apparently unaware of their dissembling attempts to hide after Eden's single rule had been broken. In the twenty-first century, however, surveillance is seldom a personal hailing, a face-to-face matter, a one-off event. It is continuous, general, routine, systematic, impersonal, and ubiquitous. It takes different forms in different parts of the world, but in places where technological dependence is deep, the surveillance of everyday life is unavoidable. In the global north we depend on it for convenience, comfort, and, especially after 9/11, we are enjoined to depend on it for security. However, the automating of surveillance facilitates new kinds of watching, which are not fully understood, let alone ethically assessed.

Not long ago I was on my way to Singapore and Hong Kong to give some lectures and attend a conference. I had no more than a slight feeling of apprehension when the pilot announced that we were to make an unscheduled landing, under directions from Air Canada. I had never before heard of such a command but I assumed, no doubt like others, that a simple explanation would be forthcoming when we landed. What did concern me at that moment was that I might miss my connection to Singapore from Vancouver. The fact that it was the morning of September 11, 2001 meant nothing at this point. It was just another day.

As soon as we landed in Winnipeg it became clear that an extraordinary event was unfolding. Strangers swapped stories of spectacular attacks on the heart of American global commerce and media in New York, and on military power at the Pentagon. Soon we were in sight of television screens that told the same unbelievable story, as they would continue to do for many days. It took a while to come to terms with the fact that I was not continuing my trip to South-East Asia at all.

Until that day I had always carried my small Swiss knife with me on trips just in case I needed one of its handy gadgets, like the tiny screwdriver for my glasses. I had nothing to hide. But when – several days later – I eventually managed to board a flight back home to Kingston, Ontario, my knife had to travel separately in an airport security envelope. There was also something unnerving about running the gauntlet of armed guards and military personnel as I made my way through the long security lines in the airport at Toronto. There was something to fear, even though, as a white male, I was not singled out for special scrutiny. As we all have discovered since, this was only the beginning.

Since then I have had my face scrutinized by intelligent cameras at Keflavik Airport in Iceland, and I have been warned of increased security because of terrorist threats by the bright new display units at Narita Airport in Tokyo. I have experienced new surveillance measures in global cities like London, Sydney, and Vienna (dogs checking carry-on at the gate), and right now I happen to be writing these words in the departure lounge at Logan Airport, Boston, from which two of those fated flights departed in September 2001. Scrutiny of baggage and of persons, from check-in to the entry ramp, is much more rigorous. I have to start up my laptop for the security guards, and show my passport photo before boarding. Airlines entering the USA are obliged to send passenger data to the destination in advance. As routine practices, all this is new.

Yet these changes are just surface symptoms of deeper and longer-term shifts in political culture, governance, and social control, not only in North America but throughout the world. True, their perceived significance differs from place to place. For instance, the national daily newspaper in Zambia granted only a couple of column inches of an inside page to the 9/11 attacks, on September 13. But there is no doubt that the events were truly global in impact. My own personal experiences, trivial troubles compared to others', are part of a bigger picture in which some public issues loom large. The task of sociology is to illuminate those connections, in this case to show how my little story finds its place within a major social transformation of the twenty-first century.

This book is about one aspect of these deeper shifts,

the surveillance initiatives that were established to try to ensure security, following the attacks. It is limited to exploring this specific dimension, although even this is complex and far-reaching in its origins and effects. It must be emphasized that while the events of 9/11 and their aftermath were unprecedented, the idea that "everything changed" on that day is highly misleading. True, Americans were brought bewilderingly face to face with foreign hatred expressed in murderous suicide assaults, and some security measures appeared that had not been there before. But many of the "deeper shifts" to which I refer were already in process, and 9/11 served simply to accelerate their arrival in a more public way.

Surveillance and Sudden Change

We can understand 9/11 – the events and their aftermath – in two ways: 9/11 may be viewed as both revealing and actually constituting major social change. The attacks brought to the surface a number of surveillance trends that had been developing quietly, and largely unnoticed, for the previous decade and earlier. Video surveillance, for example, only sporadically discussed in the mass media before then, was suddenly on everyone's lips. The idea that members of the general public could be the "ears and eyes" of security and policing services is an old one, but now it became a matter of public appeals. In other words, the establishment of "surveillance societies" that affect the lives of all ordinary people was already well under way long before 9/11. The aftermath of the attacks helps us to see more clearly what is already happening.

At the same time, the 9/11 event may also be read as an opportunity – to some, even a golden opportunity – that gave some already existing ideas, policies, and technologies their chance. In this way it helped to constitute merging social and political realities. In the USA it is clear that John Ashcroft already relished the idea of enhanced law enforcement surveillance. The desire of several governments to hold on to some semblance of social control, which some felt had been slipping away from them in a globalizing world, now found an outlet in "anti-terrorist" legislation.

Technologically, the US administration was fairly quick to come up with the astonishingly comprehensive "Total Information Awareness" scheme at the Pentagon. The data-mining technologies had been available for some time in commercial settings, but until 9/11 no plausible reason existed for deploying them – and the customer data that they analyze – within a national security appara-tus. The drive toward large-scale, integrated systems for identifying and checking persons in places such as airports and at borders, urged for years by technology companies, received its rationale as the twin towers tumbled.

As someone who has spent some time trying to docu-ment the ways in which everyday social life has come under increasingly systematic surveillance,[1] I find that 9/11 presents some fascinating and urgent challenges. Sur-veillance, as understood here, refers to routine ways in which focused attention is paid to personal details by organizations that want to influence, manage, or control certain persons or population groups. It occurs for all kinds of reasons, which can be located on a continuum from care to control. Some element of care and some element of control are nearly always present, making the process inherently ambiguous. Surveillance societies emerge wherever such practices begin to touch daily life at every point – whether we are working, shopping, voting, traveling, being entertained, or communicating with oth-ers. Responses to 9/11 are serving to speed up and spread out such surveillance in ways that bode ill for democracy, personal liberties, social trust, and mutual care.

Of course, it is all too easy to exaggerate some aspects of 9/11 in the wake of the huge media attention that has been accorded to them. Two of these should be mentioned at the start of this book. The first is that while many initiatives involve new technologies, not all surveillance is technological by any means. This book focuses particularly on the technologies, because they are the first resort, because budgets have been expanded to pay for them, and because they carry with them peculiar dangers. Yet I still stress that time-honored, direct observation is still significant. Ordinary, unmediated watching of some people by others will continue to be an important element of surveillance.

The second is that the USA is not the world. The majority of the examples in this book are American. I make no apology for this, but, as with technology, a qualification is in order. As Alan Dupont, director of the Asia-Pacific Security Program in Australia, said, "Where the U.S. goes, others will follow."[2] The USA has taken the lead in security and surveillance measures, but their lead has been followed to different degrees elsewhere. This emerges from deeper trends that the USA has in common with a number of countries (notably the UK[3]). So it is worth examining closely what happens in the USA, even if only to know what to avoid. Yet the lead of the USA is not always followed. While 9/11 and its consequences are global happenings, they are experienced locally and personally, and such experiences are different depending on circumstance. I wish to bypass the hype and to argue soberly that unless the current intensification of surveillance is slowed or stopped, in the USA and elsewhere, the emerging climate of suspicion will envelop us all in conditions that are not merely disagreeable but unjust and unfree.

What this Book is About

How does one understand surveillance today? Chapter 1 explores this question by looking at surveillance before and after 9/11. Some background is vital, so the recent history of surveillance is examined, and current theories of surveillance are reviewed to see how far they help to interpret the aftermath of the attacks. 9/11 is viewed as a prism for understanding social and political changes within surveillance societies. Existing surveillance practices are being intensified, and previous limits are being lifted on how deep or how wide the surveillance gaze may probe. After several decades in which data-protection officials, privacy watchdogs, civil rights groups, and others have tried to mitigate negative social effects of surveillance, we are witnessing a sharp tilt toward more exclusionary and intrusive surveillance practices. That this is occurring simultaneously in a number of countries as well as the most powerful, the USA, is, I shall argue, a matter of significant social concern.

The context in which this is occurring is the new global politics of terrorism. The twenty-first century is already being described breathlessly as the "age of terror" and this designation is used to justify both military and domestic policies, including security and surveillance.[4] Chapter 2 charts the intensification of surveillance, looking in particular at how "terrorism" is defined. This is a crucial question of surveillance, when "terrorists" are its target. The American Department of Homeland Security and the PATRIOT Act are but the most developed versions of anti-terrorist policy and law that have appeared since the attacks. Anti-terrorism initiatives pick up where the Cold War rhetoric and attitudes left off, replacing the old "Communist" bugbears with "terrorist" ones. I argue that compassion for victims of cold-blooded attacks and the determination to bring the perpetrators to justice is one thing; draconian dragnets based on prejudicially broad definitions of "terrorist" are quite another. The "age of terror" is turning its surveillance gaze on ordinary citizens in unprecedented and unconscionable ways. This atmosphere of suspicion is perhaps the political parallel to climate change – global chilling.

A key feature of the new security and surveillance measures is the use of high technology. A panoply of devices, including video surveillance with facial recognition, biometrics, smart ID cards, and so on, are being proposed or implemented to try to upgrade security and, so it is argued, to "prevent" future attacks. In chapter 3 I show that, quite apart from the dubious efficacy of some of these systems for stemming the spread of terrorism, their unintended consequences augur badly for the lives of ordinary citizens, especially those whose social position may already be precarious. To put this in terms of a warning to policy-makers: beware of high-technology surveillance systems that cannot achieve what their proponents claim but which may all too well curtail cherished and hard-won civil liberties.

The surveillance aftermath of 9/11 also highlights two key trends – the convergence and integration of different surveillance systems, and their globalization. The former is enabled largely by the use of increasingly similar technical methods. This is the theme of chapter 4. Techniques used in law enforcement and libraries, or in shopping and spying, use searchable databases and can also be linked to each other. Before the days of computerization, of course, such records would only be linked with special warrant, for extraordinary purposes. Today, the fact that such records are so readily available allows for easy co-option for surveillance purposes, connecting bits of data scattered across a wide range of daily activities in order to profile persons, whether as consumers or as crooks. Reactions to 9/11 have catalyzed a new phase of integrated, networked surveillance.

Such tentacle-like surveillance spreads ceaselessly not only within but also between countries. Personal data have joined the flows of images, financial transactions, and information that comprise today's globalized currents of communication. But in specific respects the volume of these flows has been expanding hugely and consequentially, especially in the global north, since 9/11. This is the theme of the fifth chapter. Three key examples are discussed: airline passenger data, already a major component of these flows, and now required on a large scale for security reasons; internet communications; and police data. Given the potential for social control of very undemocratic kinds, the lack of limits on these integrating and globalizing systems is alarming.

Of course, to comment on the growth of surveillance – especially high-technology surveillance – since 9/11 could be read as paranoid. The idea is worrying that there are massive systems designed to trace and track people, to monitor their behaviors, and to profile them – especially when the overriding motive after 9/11 is suspicion. But this is to forget that surveillance systems are themselves far from foolproof and that they also depend to a certain extent on the responses of those being surveilled. We trigger by our daily activities many surveillance devices and we also mitigate their effectiveness by negotiating or resisting them. The outcomes of post-9/11 surveillance initiatives cannot simply be seen as the result of new legal or technical measures. They emerge from complex interactions between technology and society.

There are also good reasons for questioning surveillance after 9/11. When I planned this book I had entitled the last chapter "Rethinking Surveillance," but the process of researching and writing obliged me to rethink the title itself. I have now called it "Resisting Surveillance" because I have been struck the more forcibly by the fact that the changes described are so far-reaching, retrograde, even reprehensible. There are, however, other ways forward, so as well as warning about where surveillance is going I also propose some alternatives to the panic regimes that have so far dominated responses to these events.

A central theme of the book is the culture of suspicion and how it produces and is produced by surveillance. Contemporary forms of surveillance, more than ever before, create categories of suspicion (as well as others, such as categories of seduction in consumer spheres) and these are radically reinforced after September 11. But more than this, whether new technologies are in use or not, the culture of suspicion is enlarged after 9/11, which potentially taints all reputations, and also makes surveill*ors* of us all. This is especially true in the USA but it has strong echoes elsewhere too. How this happens, however, is shrouded in secrecy. Security, we are repeatedly told, requires that information about surveillance be minimized. The upshot of this is that people are watched covertly, detained without trial and without knowledge of charges, sometimes refused lawyers, and kept incommunicado. More broadly, this reflects a reticence to be transparent about surveillance systems, a mood that collides directly with fair information practices that underlie privacy law and emerging data-protection policies worldwide. If this trend is permitted to continue unchecked, it will undermine the basic trust on which all social relationships and democratic participation depend.

I write as a sociologist, but also as a citizen. My thoughts about surveillance after 9/11 are affected not only by my research but also by personal experiences and, of course, by personal commitments. I cannot disguise my distress and indignation not only at the 9/11 attacks but also at the unjust and unnecessary military and domestic policies pursued in response. I also find myself being increasingly critical of the idolatrous reliance on high technology as savior.[5] And as a Canadian citizen I am all too aware that the activities of our closest neighbor are having a deep effect on our own security and surveillance initiatives (and this in turn inevitably colors the way that I write). Nonetheless, my experiences as an air traveler on September 11 and since remind me that security and surveillance methods are important. Governments and corporations have a responsibility to seek and secure safety for those in their care.

But many well-meaning initiatives since September 11 both fall far short of promises made for them and at the same time create new problems that will limit freedom of movement and self-determination, and augment the power and the unaccountability of governments and corporations. What I say in the following pages comes not from a merely skeptical or dissenting position, but from one that positively values what is being eroded – namely social trust, mutual care, the politics of recognition, due process, and the limits to power. Surveillance is always ambiguous; care and control are always in tension. This book argues that 9/11 is pushing the pendulum from care to control.[6]

1

Understanding Surveillance

"To be sure of apprehending criminals, it is necessary that *everyone* be supervised."

Jacques Ellul[1]

The September 11, 2001 attacks on New York and Washington prompted a series of immediate responses. They range from military retaliation in Afghanistan, the country believed to be harboring Osama Bin Laden, to extensive anti-terrorist legislation and policy aimed at domestic protection. Among the latter, one of the most prominent ongoing reactions is to enhance surveillance operations on a number of fronts. No lack of ideas has been forthcoming concerning the best way to achieve this. Very quickly, proposals were made to pour public money into policing and security services. High-tech companies fell over themselves to offer not just "heartfelt condolences" for the attack victims but technical fixes to prevent such attacks from happening again.[2] September 11 will have long-term effects in this sphere.

This chapter starts to explore the question of surveillance responses to the attacks. The background of and explanations for surveillance are probed. It begins by thinking about 9/11 as a global event and how this focuses the mind on certain crucial matters. One huge mistake, encouraged by media accounts, is to think of 9/11 as generating surveillance responses from nowhere. Just as the attacks themselves have a complex but clear context and an historical background, so too does surveillance. Jacques Ellul already noted the development of surveillance societies back in the 1960s and Orwell had inklings in the 1940s! So how did we reach the point at which everyday life is monitored so assiduously by multifarious agencies? How may the development of today's automated, dispersed surveillance be understood? And what does this all mean in the light of 9/11? As well as addressing these questions, I ask some further ones: is surveillance still centralized or not? Is its primary effect intrusion or exclusion? And is it relentless or can its effects be mitigated, deflected, or reversed? To the first two, I say, "both, and," but to the third, I say, "no, surveillance can be modified."

The Search for Meaning

The 9/11 attacks raise many important and urgent questions. With surveillance, as in many other areas, it is frequently suggested that "everything has changed," but this is manifestly not the case. The notion of change sometimes reduces to a list of new gizmos on the everyday landscape, like iris scanners at airports, and closed circuit television (CCTV) cameras on downtown streets and squares. Alternatively, it can refer to a "new era" of political control that overrides previous legal restrictions on monitoring citizens. Curiously, in this context, commentators in Britain and the USA each warned against the "police state" tactics of the other![3] But none of this, strictly speaking, is new. The underlying continuities in surveillance are at least as significant as the altered circumstances following September 11.

Despite the media hype, responses to the attacks do not amount to an entirely new surveillance landscape. Rather, already existing surveillance systems are being reinforced and intensified. They ride roughshod over the checks and balances that have been carefully developed over the past decades, and, indeed, the past couple of centuries in many western and West-influenced countries. The surveillance society was already a reality in many "democratic" countries. What 9/11 did was to produce socially negative consequences that hitherto were the stuff of repressive regimes and dystopian novels or movies. The suspension of normal conditions is justified with reference to the "war on terrorism."

What do "security" and "surveillance" mean in this context? The security sought after 9/11 builds on post-World War II notions of security, in which guarantees of inviolability and protection are sought by technical and military means as political goals. In a time of crisis guaranteed security becomes a priority that justifies placing "normal" conditions on hold. One of the key means of achieving this maximum security is through surveillance, and particularly surveillance technologies. Surveillance at its broadest means "to watch over." Sociologically, it makes sense to think in terms of paying very close attention to personal details – often in the form of digital data – for the purpose of influencing, managing, or controlling those under scrutiny.

Consider the ways in which 9/11 is a world event and what this means for social change. Focusing on the aftermath of September 11 reminds us that big events do make a difference in the social world. As Philip Abrams wisely said, an event "is a portentous outcome; it is a transformation device between past and future; it has eventuated

from the past and signifies for the future."[4] To view events
– and what is examined here, their aftermath – as important rescues our experiences in time from being merely
moments in a meaningless flux. But the event is also, says
Abrams, an "indispensable prism through which social
structure and process may be seen."[5] To see security and
surveillance issues raised to prominence, as they have been
by 9/11, is to open a window on key questions of "social
structure and process."

To take a notorious example of a world event, think of
the Holocaust. Figures such as Hannah Arendt and, perhaps more sociologically, Zygmunt Bauman,[6] have help-
fully viewed the Holocaust as revealing not merely the
human capacity for evil but also some of the key traits of
modernity itself. The triumph of meticulous rational
organization is poignantly and perversely seen in the death
camp. This makes such camps not just an inexplicable
aberration from "modern civilization," but one of its very
products. The reason that this example springs to mind in
the present context is that today's forms and practices of
surveillance, too, are products of modernity, and display a
similar ambivalence. In the case of surveillance, that which
is supposed to promote protection may actually increase
control.

The quest for security is not entirely misplaced, and
practices of surveillance are not inherently sinister or
malign. The problem is on the one hand that the notion
of maximum or guaranteed security is simply unattaina-
ble, and on the other that over-reliance on technological
surveillance carries with it some avoidable problems. At
times, the need for greater vigilance becomes apparent
and in that sense the events of September 11 acted as a
"wake-up" call. To be drowsy when dealing with danger
is downright irresponsible. But it was simultaneously a
wake-up call for those involved in the attempt to ensure

that surveillance systems are developed in appropriate and accountable ways. The attacks may have stirred surveillance experts to act decisively, but this in turn has galvanized critique and punctured complacency.

Heightened surveillance is not in itself questionable in terms of justice or freedom. In some contexts, surveillance may ensure that certain groups or individuals are *not* discriminated against. Think, for example, of the use of video cameras in police interrogation rooms, which may foster, not impede, fair treatment of suspects.[7] But in other contexts, intensified surveillance may have socially negative effects which mean that proscription takes precedence over protection, social control over mutual care. The current anxious and tense situation which has followed September 11, 2001 is helping to create a potentially parlous augmentation of surveillance of the latter kind in several countries.

Destruction and Disclosure

Images of 9/11 highlight destruction and death. To some, an era had ended; catastrophe signaled a new order. Philip Abrams' idea of events as "prisms" seems a little weak in this context, suggesting a neat reordering of light rays. This event was explosive, fiery, and fatal for more than 2000 innocent civilians. Not merely concrete and glass but a globally symbolic skyline was demolished in two strikes. The so-called "clash of civilizations"[8] seemed to have occurred as a head-on collision. For many, 9/11 was an apocalyptic event, in the sense of an unexpected and unprecedented disaster – a doomsday with almost cosmic significance. But we may also argue that 9/11 was apocalyptic in the proper sense of that term – a revelation and a judgment. This sense of apocalypse inhabits Jewish and

Christian literature, and refers more to disclosure than to destruction. The destructive dimension has to do with the alter ego of disclosure: an accounting, a turning point, a judgment.[9]

Transposing the idea of apocalypse into a sociological key, the aftermath of 9/11 may be thought of as both revealing and producing social change. That is, we may see more clearly what is going on through the 9/11 lens, but also, the aftermath of 9/11 has helped to catalyze social change. In North America "terrorism" was still seen as a relatively distant challenge until the morning of September 11, 2001, so notions of "security" and "surveillance" were not prominent in political debate. Before the dust had begun to settle amid the ruins of the World Trade Center, however, these words could be heard everywhere. Concepts such as "biometrics" and "CCTV" suddenly burst through to the foreground as proposed defenses against further attacks. The apparent crisis was immediately seen as an opportunity for already existing systems and capacities to be more fully exploited. 9/11 thus brought surveillance to the surface. The existence of a "surveillance society" became much clearer to all.

Not only did the existence of extensive surveillance systems become more obvious after 9/11, latent capacities were also realized. So although it is not the case that "everything changed" on September 11, some things definitely did. Among these was a willingness to countenance the use of certain practices – detention without trial for instance – and certain kinds of technology – say, wiretapping or internet surveillance – that were previously proscribed. The world event of 9/11 has some crucial ramifications, which, unless current trends alter, will have long-term effects throughout the twenty-first century. This is because legal and technical changes made in times of perceived crisis quickly achieve a taken-for-granted status and are subsequently very hard to dismantle. They are likely to haunt us for some time, a reckoning for which many of today's policy-makers have not bargained.

There are some even more specific ways in which the events of 9/11 relate to surveillance, understood sociologically. The attack on the World Trade Center was designed to achieve maximum media coverage. Many millions of people watched the horror unfold both during and, increasingly, after the attacks. The time delay between the assaults on the first and second of the twin towers ensured that television crews had time to get equipment in place for the spectacle to be viewed with fullest effect. This is a prime example of what Thomas Mathiesen calls the "viewer society" or the "synopticon" where the many watch the few.[10] In this case, the audience was huge, and the opportunity was exploited by repeats *ad nauseam* of the approaching jetliner, the crash into the tower, the explosion, the flames, the smoke, the pitiful people jumping to their death from windows, and the eventual terrifying collapse.

These images, in their concentrated and horribly spell-binding form, are themselves what happened on 9/11. Cut off from any antecedent history of American economic and military activities around the world, or of the growing resentment and hatred directed against the USA by a number of nations, the attacks were apparently spontaneous, utterly unexpected, and unpredictable. This made them all the more heinous in their bloody toll and their callous calculation.[11] This is the media spectacle that has its public opinion effects, which are used in turn to justify political and military responses. Those – the majority in the global north – who watched those images had their consciousness etched not just with death and destruction, but also with a particular view of the world. This view brooks little contradiction, and permits little debate. How could such awful – and awe-creating – events have happened?

The question was asked mainly in technical terms: how did US security and intelligence services not know? And it was met with a determination "not to let it happen again" – again, in primarily technical terms, but also with wide-ranging legal and policy initiatives. In actual fact, the order of these is reversed, as the next two chapters indicate. Hastily formulated legislation came first, while new technologies, though much discussed, will continue to be implemented for several years to come.

Prominent among those technical responses to 9/11 is the reinforcement of surveillance. With better systems in place, their promoters insist, the risks of another attack could be drastically reduced. With better means of identifying, classifying, profiling, assessing, and tracking the population, the chances of preventing future attacks may be increased. Such means are provided by surveillance systems, suitably automated to allow a few inspectors to watch many people. This is not the synopticon, where many watch the few, but the "panopticon" in which the few watch the many. Yet the two systems work together, the one strengthening the other.

To explain, the idea for a "panopticon" (all-seeing) prison plan came from the somewhat self-important Jeremy Bentham, a secular utilitarian social reformer in eighteenth-century England. His ideas were seen by Michel Foucault as paradigmatic of modern self-discipline under the eye of authority. Foucault supposed that the system of spectacle, tied tightly to punishment from medieval times, was being replaced in the modern world by this subtler means of social control. But against this, Mathiesen suggests that the two continue to operate together. Indeed, they do so in mutually reinforcing ways. The many watching the few does not *give way* to the few watching the many. Rather, both occur simultaneously, and both depend increasingly on similar electronic communication technologies. On 9/11 specific persons perpetrated an unprecedented attack, which could be viewed anywhere. Those acts, abstracted from previous events, generated visceral fear. They were then used to justify panic regimes and stereotypes, which in turn were fed into the freshly augmented surveillance systems, giving them both their rationale and their coded content.

Either way, of course, watching is important. This may be literal, or almost literal, in the sense of keeping watch using video surveillance. Or it may be literary – metaphorical – in the sense of monitoring personal details by other electronic means. Mediated watching has become a key feature of contemporary societies, sometimes to an obsessive degree. The popularity of so-called reality TV is some measure of this, as is the proliferation of webcams depicting mundane activities inside people's homes. Both the watching of the few by the many and the many by the few is fueled by this desire to watch – what film theorists call "scopophilia." In both cases, such scopophilia may be seen as a sort of voyeurism that reduces the rights of the watched. While reality TV show heroes may have given consent to mass viewing, others who appear on screen – such as the victims of 9/11 – have not. Equally, many who are under the panoptic gaze are not informed or have not consented to have their personal lives exposed to view.[12]

In addition to the phenomena of "watching," other aspects of social structure and process may be seen through the lens of surveillance responses to September 11. The lens helps to sharpen our focus on two matters in particular. First, the expanding range of already existing surveillance processes and practices that circumscribe and help to shape contemporary social existence, and, second, the tendency to rely on technological enhancements to surveillance systems (even when it is unclear that they work or that they speak to the problem they are established to address). However, concentrating on these two items is intended only to mitigate claims that "everything has changed" in the surveillance realm, not to suggest that nothing has changed. Indeed, the intensity and the centralization of surveillance in western countries are increasing dramatically as a result of September 11. Such systems, once in place, are harder to dismantle than to install.

The visible signs of putative changes in surveillance have both legal and technical aspects. The USA and several other countries have passed legislation intended to tighten security, to give police and intelligence services greater powers, and to permit faster political responses to "terrorist" attacks.[13] In order to make it easier to find (and to arrest) people suspected of "terrorism," typically, some limitations on wiretaps have not only been lifted but also extended to the interception of email and to internet clickstream monitoring. In Canada the Communications Security Establishment may now gather intelligence on "terrorist" groups, using "profiling" methods to track racial and national origins as well as travel movements and financial transactions. Several countries have proposed new national identification card systems, some involving biometric devices or programmable chips; others have brought forward more limited ID card systems, such as the new Canadian Permanent Resident Card[14] or the "smart ID" for asylum seekers in the UK.[15] Such systems are examined in chapter 3.

Some have questioned how new, while others have questioned how necessary, are the measures that have been fast-tracked through the legislative process. Skeptics point to the well-established UK/USA intelligence gathering agreement, for example, and to the massive message interception system once known as CARNIVORE, which already filtered millions of ordinary international email, fax, and phone messages long before September 11. Debates have occurred over how long the legal measures will be in force. The USA has a "sunset clause" that phases out the anti-terrorist law after a period of five years. Canada's law has "sunset" provisions too, but only for two items in the arsenal of new powers; detention on suspicion and interrogation before judges without the right to remain silent. But few have denied the perceived need for at least some strengthened legal framework to deal with "terrorist" threats.

Surveillance before 9/11

The surveillance systems proposed after 9/11 have the strongest possible connection with those in place before that date. In order to understand how such systems developed and became central to surveillance in the last part of the twentieth century, one has to examine in brief the story of surveillance in modern times. Surveillance is practiced with a view to enhancing efficiency, productivity, participation, welfare, health, or safety. Sheer social control is seldom a motivation for installing surveillance systems even though that may be an unintended or secondary consequence of their deployment. From the earliest days of state surveillance in sixteenth-century England, for example, the aim was to consolidate state power against others, and to maintain the position of elites, rather than to use raw informational power to keep subjects in line.[16] This is governance, not crude control.

Some might object that surveillance is as old as human society itself, and this is certainly so. People have always watched others with a view both to ensuring their safety and to checking what they are up to. Even in ancient times such practices were sometimes systematic: the biblical King David once organized a census; China operated under a central state in the 3rd century BC; imperial Rome ruled through early forms of bureaucracy; records of property transactions occurred in medieval Europe; and ever since the advent of wage labor tallies have been needed to ensure that work is properly paid for, not to mention properly done. Today's surveillance is different in the important respect that it is routine, systematic, and affects the whole population in ongoing and unavoidable ways.

Although contemporary surveillance is often seen in relation to the development of modernity,[17] central state surveillance began to appear in England – the first industrial society – early in the sixteenth century.[18] While much surveillance was local – recording births, marriages, and deaths in the parish church, administering the Poor Law, dealing with crime through justices of the peace and village constables, for instance – political and military surveillance was centralized early on. The first census, for example, taken during the Napoleonic wars, was to discover how many men were available to fight. As Edward Higgs argues, censuses were also to reassure political elites about the "vitality of the nation," not necessarily to keep tight tabs on the populace.[19] These forms of surveillance were less technologies of direct domination than the means of creating limited rights and obligations.[20] But the stage was being set for change.

In England, the modern information state really became evident in the early part of the twentieth century. In terms of both welfare and policing, the seeds were sown of central state surveillance. In one case, general police surveillance appeared in what Georg Simmel called the "society of strangers" – for registering automobiles. The

1903 Motor Car Act required vehicles to carry number plates traceable to a central registry, although at first this would of course only affect the very rich. It is interesting that this symbol of mobility – both geographic and, eventually, social, and attached even more to drivers than to vehicles – would in the post-9/11 American context become the lynch-pin in the development of a de facto national identification scheme.

Still in England, but with obvious analogies elsewhere, the combination of warfare and welfare produced much of what we now think of as the surveillance state. National mobilization for war required many kinds of record-keeping from conscription onwards. And in a well-documented twist, the requirements of peacetime were built upon that military-oriented foundation. Indeed, for a while the ID card used during the Second World War in the UK was destined to become the means of central identification for what was soon to become the National Health Service.[21]

So whereas in Victorian England the state-citizen tabs were occasional – relating to the census, birth, marriage, and death – in mid-twentieth-century England, as in all so-called advanced societies, the tabs had become multiple. Taxation, health, welfare, drivers' licenses, and other systems entail more than momentary brushes with the growing surveillance web. And the rise of foreign threats was also tied to internal threats to capitalism, especially in the Cold War. Security forces were increasingly engaged with the "enemy within," which could include labor unionists, peace activists, and minority political parties. As Higgs notes, the distinction between geopolitics and class politics was blurring.[22] Beyond this, scientific management in the workplace, and market research following on its heels, also meant that personal data was sought from and about workers and consumers.

What is referred to here as surveillance originated in

early modern times in a number of relatively discrete areas of social life, including government administration, workplace monitoring, poor relief, law and order, and military training.[23] Only as scientific management began to systematize methods of workplace control in the early twentieth century did similar surveillance methods really begin to appear in quite different settings. They also spread into new ones, such as the attempt systematically to influence customers to buy particular products through market research and advertising. By the end of the twentieth century, however, the computerization of organizational life had helped to foster an environment where more and more surveillance practices seemed similar across a widely varying social terrain.

Surveillance in capitalist workplace settings developed as an intrinsic element of this mode of production,[24] and is related in particular to what James Beniger calls the control revolution.[25] It is not doomed by this fact to produce only further exploitation. It can make for more fairness in some cases. But in many cases employees have had to struggle against the potentially oppressive aspects of workplace surveillance. Yet surveillance in the capitalist workplace is not paradigmatic for surveillance in other contexts. There is a surveillance spectrum, from hard, centralized, panoptic control to soft, dispersed, persuasion and influence. Workplace surveillance lies somewhere between the "categorical suspicion" of policing to the "categorical seduction" of consumption.[26]

Extensive computerization of administrative tasks and systems took place from the 1960s. It had the effect of reducing the burdens of cumbersome bureaucracies, but with the frequent side-effect of increasing dramatically the visibility of all citizens, workers, and, before long, consumers, through routine surveillance checks. By the 1980s and 1990s, however, this was also tied into the general economic restructuring that dismantled state welfare and radically individualized risks. Rising affluence and mobility also increased opportunities for crime and deviance, which in turn fostered an emerging "culture of control."[27] It is important to put these matters in their broad social context, rather than viewing them as some kind of conspiracy of the powerful.

Much of the mushrooming growth of surveillance in twentieth-century administration and commerce may be related to "disappearing bodies." Rising rates of mobility, coupled with the stretching of social relationships enabled by new technologies of travel and communications, meant that fewer and fewer transactions and interactions are based on face-to-face relationships. It's not that we have forsaken face-to-face relationships with friends, family, and colleagues, but rather that we simply never see many of those with whom we interact via card-reading machines, phones, email, and so on. This produces a quest for means of compensation with what can be called "tokens of trust."[28] Hence the PINs, bar-codes, signatures, and, eventually, photo IDs and biometrics that lace the cards we carry. Human beings, embodied persons, are thus abstracted from place and are siphoned as data into flows, to be reconstituted as "data images" in surveillance systems. Multifarious systems developed from the 1960s onwards, some of which had links but in general (and partly due to legal constraint) few opportunities to trace across databases without specific cause.

Theorizing the Surveillance Gaze

In order to get a handle on surveillance developments after 9/11, it is not enough to describe changes; some kind of interpretation or explanation is needed. Various such theoretical resources are available, each of which throws some light on current events. If we place the emphasis on capitalism, then clearly surveillance is likely to be in service for the purpose of retaining control over employees and resources, while freeing as far as possible the conditions of trade. Exploitative relationships, engendered by capitalism, are perpetuated using the tools available, including surveillance. In the workplace, surveillance is often an arena of conflict, and outcomes are contested and negotiated.[29] But if bureaucracy is highlighted, then some features of surveillance are seen that go beyond capitalist relations; the rationalization and attempted control of more and more life-spheres certainly carry with them heightened surveillance, but also a sense of radical insecurity. As global modernization produces more risks, so more efforts are made to counteract risk, particularly through insurance based on surveillance information.[30]

These perspectives offer important insights into today's surveillance situations, although they do have to be constantly checked against current developments. For example, both "capitalist society" and "bureaucracy" theories appeared in the late nineteenth or early twentieth centuries and tended to deflect attention from a parallel process of individualization.[31] Thus in the capitalist context we see today the individualization both of work[32] and also of consumption. The marketer's dream is to target not only "niches" but eventually to lure individuals into purchasing specific items, using data on their lifestyles and preferences gleaned by surveillance. But "risk," too, is being individualized, especially as the old communal means of sharing risks – such as the welfare state – are being scaled down. Within welfare itself, surveillance is searching and severe,[33] but beyond it, every agency seeks more and more detailed records of health, performance, income, and other personal data.

Whatever sociologists have to say, it would be foolish to ignore the one name that is always invoked in surveillance studies: George Orwell. His novel, *Nineteen Eighty-Four*, and its monstrous anti-hero, Big Brother, have become bywords within the surveillance genre. And with good reason. Orwell noted the deformation of language as well as the use of technologies – such as the ubiquitous two-way "telescreen" – to mediate surveillance, and he also maintained a subtle ambivalence about whether his work was aimed at state socialist or liberal democratic societies. While many in the western world smugly imagined that his critique exposed Communist regimes in the then "Iron Curtain" countries, much of what he predicted about surveillance is actually true of liberal democracies. And while he could not have imagined the extent to which electronic technologies would facilitate surveillance, or that they would be used as much in the consumer as the citizenship sphere (or, for that matter, that citizenship would increasingly resemble consumption), his warnings are well taken.

Theoretically, what George Orwell feared was a state-organized central surveillance apparatus, a pyramid of power in which ruler and ruled were transparent to each other. Although other aspects of surveillance were significant by the 1970s, it was to this centralized model that the earliest sociological study of contemporary surveillance referred, as the archetypical avoidable future.[34] Such studies looked to Max Weber and his followers as well, of course, with his focus on record-keeping, files, hierarchies of control, and knowledgeable officials, all of which are important for understanding bureaucratic surveillance. The question did begin to present itself, however: would the increasing use of computers to buttress bureaucratic procedures itself make a difference to how surveillance was done? In earlier studies, computerization was seen

mainly as a means of augmenting already existing processes. Today, questions have been raised as to whether
computerization produces new forms of "discursive"
power.[35]

As electronic forms of surveillance became more widely
distributed, however, many turned to Foucault's treatment of Bentham's panopticon as a means of considering
ubiquitous power based on continuous observation. It is
partly a centralized scheme, though there is scope for its
localization into the "capiliary" levels in the minutiae of
everyday life. Such centralized surveillance always brings
with it the risk of totalitarianism,[36] but checks and balances, and the vigilance of privacy lobbies, labor unions,
civil rights movements, and consumer groups, have traditionally proved quite effective in curbing it, especially in
the West.

There is more to the panoptic idea than meets the eye,
however. Indeed, the "eye" is in some ways central to the
lively debate.[37] As we saw earlier, some argue that the
"synoptic" eye of the many watching the few is just as
important as the "panoptic" eye of the few watching the
many. But there is another significant debate between
those who consider that the "unseen observer" is the key
feature of the panoptic, especially as this seems to reflect
the highly unobtrusive forms of electronic data-gathering
available today, and those who argue that the classificatory
powers of the panoptic are what really define it.[38] In the
latter view, the panopticon may be seen in many settings
from police work to database marketing.[39] With regard to
9/11, the proliferation of new surveillance technologies
does mean that the surveillance "eye" is less easy to
discern. Yet the use of searchable databases – especially
for profiling – means that the classificatory powers of the
panoptic are heightened. Such profiling has occurred
especially along "racial" lines, focusing on "Arab" popu-

lations in particular. "Middle Eastern" students, for instance, were singled out in an FBI trawl of more than 200 US campuses.[40]

In recent years, interest in the centralized panoptic or Orwellian variants of the surveillant apparatus has been depleted somewhat as the notion of a surveillant assemblage has attracted the attention of theorists. The latter idea originates in the fertile imagination of Gilles Deleuze,[41] and has been pursued fruitfully by a number of social scientists,[42] not least because it seems to account for the dispersal, decentralization, and globalization of surveillance. The assemblage, in this context, is a set of loosely linked systems, to be distinguished from the operation of government, at least as classically understood by political scientists. It is emergent and unstable. It operates across state institutions and others that have nothing (directly) to do with the state. From the viewpoint of the data-subject, this relates to our daily experiences of surveillance, which occur in mundane moments rather than in special searches. As Nikolas Rose puts it, "surveillance is 'designed in' to the flows of everyday existence."[43]

A key example is insurance categories used by police to determine risk, or, in the post-9/11 situation, using consumer as well as police and intelligence data to profile persons at borders to calculate their potential threat. The assemblage is all about linking, cross-referencing, pulling threads together that previously were separate. This also hints at its mode of growth. It is like the weed "Creeping Charlie" that sends out horizontal shoots which in turn become new nodes in a constantly growing network. It is, as Gilles Deleuze and Felix Guatarri would say, "rhizomic." In the assemblage, surveillance works by abstracting bodies from places and splitting them into flows to be reassembled as virtual data-doubles, calling in question once again hierarchies and centralized power.

One important aspect of this is that the flows of personal and group data percolate through systems that once were much less porous; much more discrete and watertight. Thus, following September 11, surveillance data from a myriad of sources – supermarkets, motels, traffic control points, credit card transaction records, and so on – were used to trace the activities of the "terrorists" in the days and hours before their attacks. The use of searchable databases makes it possible to use commercial records previously unavailable to police and intelligence services and thus draws on all manner of apparently "innocent" traces.

From what we have seen of surveillance after 9/11, however, it is wrong to imagine that the loosely networked assemblage simply supplants the centralized apparatus. Indeed, Deleuze and Guatarri themselves distinguish between different kinds of rhizome, some of which allow for continued hierarchical control. The rising tide of risk management techniques has indeed flooded over old distinctions between different institutional areas, but instability is endemic. Outcomes are impossible to predict. True, "organized risk management" was somewhat eclipsed by "disorganized" and "disorderly" systems in the last part of the twentieth century.[44] But state forms of surveillance have by no means disappeared, and a world event like 9/11 has shown that they have both power and influence when perceived threats are of a sufficient magnitude. The assemblage and the apparatus are overlapping, even superimposed and mutually informing systems, and the assemblage can still be appropriated by the apparatus. Indeed, this is so partly because governments have increasingly taken their cue from risk management – they themselves are changing their character as they do so. We shall explore this further in chapter 4.

This brief survey[45] of surveillance shows how the once-dominant model of centralized state informational power has been challenged by socio-technical developments. So new models incorporate the growth of information and communication technologies in personal and population data-processing. And there are more networked modes of social organization with their concomitant flexibility and departmental openness. But other kinds of explanation may not be jettisoned with impunity, as if they were simply rendered redundant by social change. To illustrate this, I shall simply offer a series of questions that once again allow the prism of the September 11 aftermath to point up aspects of structure and process that relate in particular to surveillance.

Critical Questions

Three critical questions may be asked of surveillance developments since 9/11. Much hangs on the answer to each one.

The first is this: is surveillance best thought of as centralized power or dispersed assemblage? The responses to September 11 are a stark reminder that for all its changing shape since World War II, the nation-state is still a formidable force, especially when the apparently rhizomic shoots can still be exploited for very specific purposes to tap into the data they carry. The Big Brother trope did not in its original incarnation refer to anything outside the nation-state (such as the commercial or internet surveillance that is prevalent today). Nor did Orwell guess at the extent to which the "telescreen" would be massively enhanced by developments first in microelectronics and then in communications including global TV and searchable databases. But it would be naive to imagine that Big Brother type threats are somehow a thing of the past.

Draconian measures are appearing worldwide as country after country instates laws and practices purportedly to counter "terrorism." US Attorney General John Ashcroft warned Patrick Leahy, one of the only American senators seriously to raise his voice against the new police powers, that "talk won't prevent terrorism."[46] Panic responses such as these, that both silence critical discussion and impose restrictions on civil liberties through policing and security crackdowns, are likely to have long-term and possibly irreversible consequences. They permit extraordinary "wartime" measures, which include appropriating data on everyday communications and transactions – phone calls, email, the internet – while implicitly discouraging the use of these media for democratic debate. The surveillant assemblage is being co-opted for conventional "strong state" purposes.

Secondly, with regard to the experience of surveillance it is worth asking: is intrusion or exclusion the key motif? Today's societies of the global north have undergone processes of steady privatization. The social world is all too often conceived as a series of bubbles of personal space. So it is not surprising that surveillance is often viewed in individualistic terms as a potential threat to privacy, an intrusion into an intimate life, an invasion of the sacrosanct home (women and men may see this one differently), or as jeopardizing anonymity. While all these are understandable attitudes (and ones that invite their own theoretical and practical responses), none really touches one of the key aspects of contemporary surveillance: "social sorting."[47] It is hard to get an adequate theoretical handle on this, and no compelling metaphor – such as "Big Brother" – has yet been proposed to give it popular cachet.

The increasingly automated discriminatory mechanisms for risk profiling and social categorizing represent a key means of reproducing and reinforcing social, economic, and cultural divisions in informational societies. They tend to be highly unaccountable, especially in contexts such as video surveillance.[48] This is why the common promotional refrain, "if you have nothing to hide, you have nothing to fear" is vacuous. Categorical suspicion has consequences for anyone, "innocent" or "guilty," caught in its gaze, a fact that has poignant implications for the new anti-terror measures enacted after September 11. It is already clear in several countries that Arab and Muslim minorities are disproportionately and unfairly targeted by these measures.

The experience of surveillance also raises the third question of how far subjects collude with, negotiate, or resist practices that capture and process their personal data? Surveillance is not merely a matter of the gaze of the powerful, any more than it is technologically determined. Data-subjects interact with surveillance systems. As Foucault says, we are "bearers of our own surveillance," but it must be stressed that this is not merely an unconscious process in which we are dupes. Surveillance is always ambiguous. There are genuine benefits and plausible rationales as well as palpable disadvantages. So the degree of collaboration with surveillance depends on a range of circumstances and attitudes. Under the present panic regime, it appears that anxious publics are willing to put up with many more intrusions, interceptions, delays, and questions than was the case before September 11. This process is amplified by media polarizations of the "choice" between "liberty" and "security."[49] The consequences of this complacency could be far-reaching. But things do not have to remain this way. These three critical questions do not exhaust what might be said of surveillance after 9/11. They are merely a starting point for assessment. A further, and deeper, theme that will emerge in what follows connects the social analysis with the normative in important ways. It may be stated as a question: can merely instrumental, rationalized approaches to governance – such as the reliance on law and technology – be sustained in the long term? Are there social limits to technical solutions? As we shall see, such technical solutions dominate discussion. But their effects are to create not less but more fear and uncertainty. They rachet up the stakes in an ever-rising spiral. They become self-perpetuating at the same time as public commitment drains away from them. It seems that at a certain point they lose their social moorings and end up exacerbating the situations they were intended to address.

Running through this book, then, is another critical question about the limits of legal and technical measures. This means going beyond the approaches that focus on "rationalization" to explore the ways that technologies are embedded in everyday social life. It means asking if societies in the global north are in danger of forgetting the importance of informal associations, moral communities, and communicational rituals which are surely the counterpoint to radical rationalization.[50] This in turn begs the question of mutual trust, which would appear to be at a low premium in the suspicious climate of today's terrorist fears. And thus exploring the ways in which the ethics of justice has to be tempered with an ethics of caring,[51] and in which trust becomes a central motif, is a vital task ahead.

Prisms, Perspectives, and Practices

Surveillance responses to September 11 are indeed a prism through which aspects of social structure and process may be observed. The prism helps to make visible the already existing vast range of surveillance practices and processes that touch everyday life in so-called informational societies. And it helps to check various easily made assumptions about surveillance – that it is more dispersed than centralized, that it is more intrusive than exclusionary, that data-subjects are dupes of the system, that it is technically driven, that it contributes more to prevention than to investigation after the fact.

As we have seen, none of these assumptions is correct. After 9/11 the surveillance *state* shows itself to be stronger than ever, even though it now uses the dispersed systems and devices of surveillance *society*. The latter even include retooled techniques of high-tech marketing to root out "terrorists." Despite frequent fears of invaded privacy, intrusion into private lives is not the biggest problem associated with surveillance. The effects of surveillance are to discriminate and to exclude the suspicious category. It reinforces social distinctions and divisions. Intrusion is merely a by-product of this. Yet data-subjects – any and all of us who are caught in the surveillance gaze – are not dupes. We often participate in our own surveillance, simply by walking along downtown streets, using telephones and bank machines, by accepting loyalty cards from stores and express cards for frequent flyers. We can say no – and many do. Surveillance is not technology-driven either, even though faith in technology remains strong. Surveillance is technologically augmented on a daily basis, but this is the outcome of commercial decisions and government policy as it was prior to 9/11. Its effect, however, is less to anticipate and prevent crime or violence than to increase the stock of analyzable information.

So caution seems to be called for in seeing older, modernist models of surveillance simply as superseded by newer, late- or postmodern ones. For all its apparent weaknesses in a globalizing world, the nation-state is capable of quickly tightening its grip on internal control. And it uses means that include the very items of commercial surveillance – phone calls, supermarket visits, and internet surfing – that appear "soft" and scarcely worthy of inclusion as "surveillance." Astonishingly, for all the doubts cast on the risk-prone informational, communications, and transport environment, naive faith in the promise of technology seems undented by the "failures" of September 11.

Surveillance responses to 9/11 have a history, just as the attacks themselves do. Surveillance was already moving steadily in the direction of systematic social sorting, long before surveillance attention was focused on profiling Arabs and Muslims. And the surveillance systems predating 9/11 continue to operate, sifting the socially acceptable from the rest and filtering the feckless for closest scrutiny. It's just that now another set of criteria configure part of the grid. Combing the data for terrorists simply adds another dimension to the categories of suspicion and the relations of risk. This calls for vigilance on more than one front. The loss of civil liberties entailed in the war on terrorism is worth warning about, but not at the expense of forgetting that some groups were already discriminated against using surveillance techniques. It would be easy to be distracted from the struggle against surveillance-assisted inequality by the dramatic developments in the currently media-magnified arena of regimes of terror.

To understand surveillance before and after 9/11, then, close attention must be paid to history and to political economy. Only these will help us grasp the systemic and structural aspects of surveillance today. These items are necessary, but they are not sufficient. In addition, normative approaches are vital. These inform and breathe life into analysis. Today's surveillance is increasingly computer-assisted and technology-dependent. This means that the reinforcement and reproduction of social inequalities are being automated. In such conditions it is easy to lose sight of real people in the real world, but it is for their sake that surveillance should be democratically decided upon and assessed by high standards of justice *and* care.

In the current climate it is hard to see how calls for democratic accountability and ethical scrutiny of surveillance systems will be heard as anything but liberal whining. Yet democratic accountability begins with a willingness to listen to the voice of the other. And ethical scrutiny starts with care for the other, to relieve and to prevent suffering. The sociology of surveillance discussed above sees neglect of these as a serious mistake, with ramifications we may all live to regret.

2

Intensifying Surveillance

"... we may look back, I fear, to see this as the beginning of something even worse."

Margaret Drabble[1]

Times of crisis generate extraordinary measures. War, in particular, produces tightened security on the home front and the temporary suspension of some civil rights. After the attacks on America on 9/11, a "war on terrorism" was declared by the US President George Bush, and along with it a supposed choice was offered: security or liberty. The dream of guaranteed security, developed in the last part of the twentieth century, was now used to justify extraordinary measures, which include the intensification of surveillance. These political, legal, technical moves affect not only all Americans, but also many in the global north, along with other populations across the face of the earth. The ideals of living in a free, fair, and fraternal society are in question in the aftermath of 9/11.

During the latter half of the twentieth century, definitions of "war" broadened somewhat. Without doubt, the twentieth was the bloodiest war-ridden century in human history but after its second *world* war a "Cold War" developed between the American and Soviet superpowers.

Other "wars" were also declared, notably in Britain, where offensives were declared against want, ignorance, disease, and so on. But the wars against unacceptable living conditions involved no loss of liberties. The Cold War, however, involved threats, suspicion, and surveillance of enemies within, a massive development and deployment of computer-power,[2] and, eventually, a scenario of "mutually assured destruction." The American McCarthyism of the period was notorious for its stereotyping of "Communist agitators" and its irresponsible and risible "reds under the bed" scare tactics. Mercifully, the Cold War came to an end in 1989 with the symbolic dismantling of the Berlin Wall.

Unfortunately, neither real wars nor surrogate ones came to an end at that time. Among other things, the US announced a "War on Drugs" to try to cut supplies of illicit substances. This attempt to deter drug use also involves surveillance, including methods such as wiretaps.[3] After September 11, 2001 the War on Drugs was eclipsed by another, which is now far more familiar. As with the drug war, The War against Terrorism escalates legal and technical counter-measures in an apparently ongoing spiral. The new powers address not only suspected terrorists but other kinds of crime as well, yet this is a war whose location and timing is unclear. Terrorists live among urban civilian populations, so attacking them, as Gwynne Dyer says, is like declaring war on carpentry.[4] It is also a war-without-end because terrorism is likely to be an ongoing threat.

This chapter explores three issues. The first concerns suspicion. The backwash from 9/11 is inundating citizens in the global north and elsewhere under waves of suspicion. The culture of suspicion is not new, but 9/11 has deepened it. Its crucial new element comprises legal definitions of "terrorist" which serve to identify surveillance

targets. This in turn strengthens police powers and intelligence operations. The second issue is secrecy. Uncannily, H. G. Wells more than hinted at this in his sci-fi
story of New York aerial attacks, *The War in the Air*,
published in 1908: "One of the most striking facts histor-
ically about this war, and one that makes complete the
separation between the methods of warfare and democracy, was the effectual secrecy of Washington."[5] This is
tragically true of today's "war on terrorism," and not only
near Washington. One thing that is no secret, however, is
the third issue: mobilizing citizens as spies. Not content
with placing newly defined "terrorists" under suspicion,
the new regime also recasts ordinary people as surveillors.
Before turning to these three questions, a few preliminary
comments are called for on why civil liberties are important, and on who are the real victims.

Visible Victims; Fading Freedoms

Civil liberties have fallen on hard times since 9/11. New
laws and technologies disregard or deny them. They are
easy to demolish, difficult to repair. The much-cherished
belief in the fairness of a society in which opportunities
are reputedly open to all has also been tarnished since
9/11. New York's other famous symbol, the Statue of
Liberty, must weep on her stand. True, the USA never
has managed to live up to its noble claim to be a society
of equality. But since the events of 2001, already existing
inequalities and disadvantage are set to be reinforced. In
wartime, hostile defenses are raised against the Other, the
enemy, and a culture of suspicion emerges, from which
no one is exempt. This "war" is no exception. Mutual
trust, the bedrock of sociality, is thus being undermined.

It is worth recalling where "civil liberties" came from.

They are the product of considerable struggle in the modern era, and are closely connected with a number of rights that have been built up over 200 years and more.[6] Civil rights guarantee fair treatment for individuals before the law, and have to do with the freedom to live where you choose, to own property, and to hold religious beliefs and speak freely. In the USA, political rights – to participate in public elections and to run for office – spread from property-owners to all white men, to women, to black people – but not without a fight. Social rights – to minimum standards of living and economic security – were a product of twentieth-century welfare states, which are now waning in most countries where they were established. In 1948, as a result of the brutal racism and contempt for life of the Holocaust, these were summed up in the International Declaration of Human Rights that included the right to life, liberty, and security of the person, the recognition everywhere of a person before the law, and freedom of movement.

After September 11, all the focus was on punctured security. The borders of the safe haven, the "land of the free", had been breached. "Outrage!" screamed a Canadian headline on the morning after, echoing the sense of affront south of the border that the superpower should become the "victim."[7] Given the opportunity to realize what kind of world it was part of, as Slavoj Žižek says, the USA refused this chance, choosing instead to reassert its traditional ideological commitments: "out with feelings of responsibility and guilt towards the impoverished Third World, *we* are the victims now!"[8] This became clearer than ever in Canada when the prime minister, Jean Chretien, had the temerity to suggest that the wealthy western world had helped to create the conditions for terrorism through its relationship with poorer countries. "You cannot exercise your powers to the humiliation of

others," he said in a speech on the first anniversary of 9/
11. He was savaged by the American TV networks.[9] The
official US pose was that of a sorrowing victim.

The world was quickly realigned in simple binary terms:
for or against the USA. Security was in; liberty was out.
Grief, perfectly genuine, of course, but exploited ideolog-
ically, was powerfully combined with victim status. This
gave an easy rationale to those who saw the opportunity
to shore up the power of the police and the intelligence
services, not to mention the chance to demonstrate US
military might in Afghanistan. On the one hand, there was
a shameful sense that something had slipped out of control. On the other, a sense that between the quickly
forming camps was a gray area of potential enemies –
suspects. Regaining and reinforcing control became an
instant priority, alongside its twin, creating, or confirming,
a culture of suspicion.

Something deeply anti-political imbues the new security
measures. Franz Neumann avers that as the language of
security and risk becomes dominant the social and legal
context of individual behavior, and thus of political bar-
gaining, is increasingly stripped away.[10] One could also
observe that the attempt to minimize political debate has
been present for a long time, even in the US Constitution
and the Bill of Rights. The effective denial of popular
sovereignty simply reappeared after 9/11, suggests Will
Hutton, and this was seen in John Ashcroft's permitting
private military trials, the execution of non-Americans
deemed to be terrorists, and the widespread resumption
of wiretapping telephone calls and emails. As Hutton says,
"the scale of this withdrawal of civil liberties to combat
terrorism is excessive and hard to justify in terms of
potential results." Yet by April 2003 some congressional
Republicans were trying to make the anti-terrorism laws
permanent.[11]

The cultures of control and of suspicion were not new departures after 9/11. They simply snowballed after that date, fueled by the fear, anger, and grief of "victims" and by the political pose of retaliation. These cultures had already been developing during the latter part of the twentieth century. Political participation was already being eclipsed by risk management, which profiles populations as a means to control and erodes civil liberties. Risk regimes were already producing the crucial categories of suspicion within which individuals may be located but where their voice is muted. But in two crucial respects, legal and technological, the cultures of control and suspicion were given a boost after 9/11.

New legislation and policy have an impact on any who might choose to dissent from the dominant view, particularly protesters, labor unions, academics, and religious groups. A chilling effect occurs, which is made the more icy by the secrecy that surrounds some significant cases. You don't have to be a dissident to be under suspicion. New laws and policies turn everyone into a potential suspect or into a potential ally of the FBI or the CIA. Note that these forms of surveillance need no computer networks or biometric identifiers.

Capturing "Terrorists":
A Culture of Suspicion

The 9/11 attacks galvanized the US administration into action. Within a month, new anti-terror legislation – the PATRIOT Act – had been passed to deal with police powers, courts, and the treatment of suspects. In just over a year a new department – Homeland Security – had been set up and was in operation. The federal Department of Homeland Security now has the unprecedented mandate of helping to prevent, protect against, and respond to acts of terrorism on American soil.[12] But it was not only in the USA that such steps were taken. Many countries responded to the attacks with legislation and new policies of their own. These included Canada and Mexico (immediately fingered as borders porous to the flow of terrorists), several European and South-East Asian countries, Australia, South Korea, and Japan.

The flurry of legislative activity that occurred in many countries after 9/11 was intended among other things to close legal loopholes through which terrorists might escape. In fact, it fit a familiar pattern that has emerged over the past 30 years or so, of attempting to calculate, prepare for, and, if possible, pre-empt risk. Contemporary societies produce risks on a large scale, just because they intervene so decisively in natural and social life, using a range of technologies to do so.[13] Managing risk is now central to government activity. Since the Cold War era in the 1950s and 1960s, the dominant view was that security against the risk of foreign aggression (of Soviet power against the USA) could be guaranteed by technical and military means. Security technologies have proliferated, and with them two central beliefs: one, the idea that "maximum security" is a desirable goal; and, two, that it can be pursued using these increasingly available techniques that are on the market.

What was seen previously as a minor risk to North America suddenly became a bloody reality: terrorists could strike with deadly accuracy at the most prized symbols of American global prowess. In an instant, military forces had to be put on full alert, quickly followed by notice of legislative change and technical upgrading of security. Existing arrangements to cope with risk were seen as inadequate and flawed and new calculations were made, especially in relation to where the security walls had been breached, in airports, at borders, and in the passing of messages to do with the plot.

Ironically, these places of high risk as danger are also places of high risk as economic adventure. Today's world is dominated by flows of capital, technology, persons, and information. What made the WTC such a soaring symbol of American pride was precisely that it encapsulated the global networks of commerce enabled by new technologies. Somehow protection had to be found in the same world of mobility, of flows, in which the goal of unfettered free movement now had to be countered with filters, checks, and other sorting mechanisms. "Anti-terrorism" is now at the top of political agendas. Governments throughout the world strive to show that they are doing something. Their actual achievement is to increase airport security and to pass anti-terrorism laws. How far these will succeed in their stated aims is another matter.

Much sound and fury has been evident, but what this signifies is more moot. As we shall see, some of the technical innovations are hardly foolproof, and persuading different offices and departments to work in unison is no simple task either. The experiences of the USA are also matched elsewhere. To the chagrin of some at a Canadian Bar Association meeting in August 2002, for example, two major issues were outstanding: civil liberties have suffered unnecessarily under anti-terrorist law "Bill C-36" and Canadian intelligence-gathering is no more integrated or coordinated than that in the USA, where the CIA and FBI remain as "separate islands of intelligence."[14]

This sense that the intelligence-gathering organizations failed is partly behind the new legislation passed in several countries in the aftermath of 9/11. One year later, reports emerged of warnings as far back as 1998 that "Arab terrorists" might use bomb-laden planes to attack the WTC. However, these were not taken seriously by the

FBI or the Federal Aviation Administration.[15] The scramble-speed laws were intended to plug such security dykes. Thus police and intelligence services were granted new powers, and technical capacities to create databases on citizens were augmented. It became easier to eavesdrop on conversations, and, significantly, fresh efforts were made to define the word "terrorist." The matter of definition is crucially important. Once some activity is thought of as "terrorism," then surveillance powers aimed at such groups are justified. As the American Civil Liberties Union (ACLU) noted, terrorism was defined in the first draft of the PATRIOT Act such that it could include simple civil disobedience of a kind used by People for the Ethical Treatment of Animals (PETA).[16]

In the USA, the PATRIOT Act – "Uniting and Strengthening America by Providing Appropriate Tools Required to Intercept and Obstruct Terrorism" – was passed by a huge majority in October 2001. Since then, police powers have grown, courts have been bypassed, and suspects have been held in prison indefinitely without the public being informed as to who they are or even how many there are. Australia's new law requires persons to provide "information, records, or things" to authorities, puts the onus on the accused to prove their innocence, and makes it possible for people to "disappear" or to be held incommunicado. In Canada, Bill C-36 introduced dragnet police powers such as detention without charge and compelled testimony before a judge.[17] Such changes in practice and in law have also occurred in Austria, Britain, Denmark, France, Germany, India, Singapore, and Sweden.

Who Is a Terrorist?

One key issue is the definition of "terrorism" which until 9/11 had been largely covered by other words and phrases. The word terrorism is notoriously slippery, not least because one person's "freedom fighter" is another's "terrorist." One only has to consider Protestant/Catholic troubles in Northern Ireland, the African National Congress struggles against Apartheid in South Africa, or Israeli-Palestinian conflicts to see how this is so. The process whereby victims are depicted in the popular media as terrorists is not complex or arcane. The image can all too easily dominate the facts.[18] But the issue revolves around who may be included in this definition, not merely its contested designation. The PATRIOT Act depends on a new definition of terrorism, as do other laws around the world. Most people would agree that violent and arbitrary actions with a political aim that are deliberately aimed at civilians would count as terrorism. But much more than this lurks in the new laws against terrorism.

The PATRIOT Act defines terrorism as "criminal acts dangerous to human life committed principally within the United States that appear to be intended to coerce a civilian population or to influence a governmental policy by intimidation or coercion or to affect the conduct of a government by mass destruction, assassination, or kidnapping." According to the Act, "threatening, conspiring or attempting to hijack . . .," representing or seeking support for a terrorist group, or being a family member – unless it can be proved that you have "renounced terrorism" – makes one a terrorist.

The European Union's "Framework Decision" on combating terrorism, which came into force on January 1, 2003, also has a broad definition that includes damage to installations – such as information infrastructures – or institutions, and assumes an "aim of seriously altering political, economic, or social structure."[19] Not only this, but measures will also be taken to suppress "any form of support, active or passive, to entities or persons involved in terrorist acts."[20] Similarly, in Canada, Bill C-36 extends terrorism to include those "who intend to cause serious interference with or serious disruption of an essential service" and it also permits a Minister to compile a list of "terrorist groups."

With definitions as broad as this, it is clear that all kinds of activity may be branded as "terrorist," including what were previously perfectly lawful demonstrations or protests. The net of social control is thus stretched to include many unsuspecting figures within its reach. This is not new either, but 9/11 has intensified the process. For instance, it was revealed recently that the police in Denver, Colorado, have been collecting information on local activists since the 1950s. They transferred the data from little index cards to a computer system from Orion Scientific Systems, which stores, searches, and categorizes it. Some groups, including the American Friends Service Committee, a Nobel Peace Prize winner, and individuals such as an elderly nun who taught "destitute Indians," were listed as "criminal extremists."[21] Since computerization occurred, data had also been shared with other departments. Orion began life with a Defense Advanced Research Projects Agency (DARPA) project and now boasts on its web site of new anti-terrorist capacities.[22]

But it is not only "terrorism" that is broadly defined. Practices known as "profiling" are also permitted under new legislation. Usually this is "racial" profiling, involving the category of "Muslim-Arab." With approximately 1.2 billion Muslims in the world, it is not clear how this "narrows" the categories of suspicion, but this is just the point: it does not. Rather, a means has been obtained of widening the net even further, with results that have already been seen in several countries.[23] It is hard to escape Frank Furedi's cynical conclusion that "terrorists become any people you don't like."[24] The widening of the "terrorist" definition means not only that dissenting, or even doing nothing, might spark suspicion, but that altruistic activities, particularly among Muslims, may also come under scrutiny. Many Muslim immigrants to North America (and elsewhere) send money back to their country of origin, to support families or charities. But they have become more reluctant to do so since the post-9/11 freezing of assets. In the long term, quite apart from the direct distress caused by unwanted attention, such restrictions could further exacerbate the growing divide between global north and south.

Given the draconian nature of these legal changes, it is surprising that more opposition to these laws was not voiced as they were being enacted. Yet the PATRIOT Act, and others akin to it, was passed very quickly, and with minimal opportunity for debate. Constitutional rights seem at a low premium and taken-for-granted civil liberties are being eroded. Some dissent has been expressed, but in the USA this was muted. The reasons are not hard to find. The emotional mood of national sorrow maintained by the media plays a part, as does the fact that President Bush declared in a pre-emptive strike that those not against the terrorists were with the terrorists. Since then, however, criticism has, if anything, mounted. In Europe serious questions are being raised about new laws, with the organization Statewatch[25] becoming a key source of information. In the USA during 2002, several cities defied the PATRIOT Act, instructing police not to comply with all its directives. The cities include Ann Arbor, Berkeley, and Cambridge.[26]

Capturing terrorists before they strike became an obsessive goal of many governments after 9/11. In order to pursue this goal, laws were passed with broad and, in the end, unworkable definitions of terrorism, and with permission to profile populations in ways that are unlikely to pinpoint a potential aggressor. However, these laws are not without effect. They put back the clock of civil rights. And they create webs of suspicion that are neither warranted nor, in most cases, worthy of the governments that have started to spin them. However, another factor enters the picture once the laws are enacted: transparency is reduced, such that some arrests, charges, and detentions can occur – and are occurring, without public knowledge. Not only is a culture of suspicion emerging; a culture of secrecy is emerging alongside it.

A Chilly Climate: The Culture of Secrecy

The combined effect of the anti-terrorism laws enacted since 9/11 is to create a cool climate for many activities well beyond that of "terrorism." The chilling effect of these laws affects first those who have actually been detained since 9/11, both within the USA and, notoriously, in Guantanamo Bay, Cuba. In the latter, a US base apparently beyond the reach of either the Geneva Convention or the American Constitution, 564 "suspected members of Al Qaeda" of 39 nationalities were being held in 2002 for "interrogation."[27] But on the US mainland, as well, about 1,200 persons have also been held for their potential involvement in terrorist activities. Little is known about these people except that they are considered part of an insidious enemy within.

Similar difficulties have arisen in other countries too. For example, a Canadian engineer from Ottawa, Maher

Arar, was recently deported to Syria by US immigration officials while changing planes in New York on his way home from vacation. It transpired that wrong data in an FBI database, linking him to terrorism, had never been removed. A family visit to Tunisia, to visit his wife's parents and to introduce them to their new grandchild, was the source of the misunderstanding. One can only conclude that due process was denied.[28]

The chilling effect arises not only from the lack of due process, a basic civil right, accorded to "suspects" since 9/11. It also arises from the ways in which laws and policies are affecting particular groups within the populations of affected countries. Why were federal investigators found in universities and colleges across America checking on students from Middle Eastern countries between September and December 2001? Because one of the 9/11 attackers apparently had a student visa. This was justification enough for checking on the half-a-million foreign students in the USA. The visits were unannounced, and most universities complied – even if reluctantly – because they seemed to have no option in law.[29] And why have employers been securing the services of private investigators to help with hiring processes since 9/11? Because anyone may now pose a "security risk" not revealed on the resumé.[30] So the chilling effect seeps into the production plant, the classroom, the store, and the office.

As the chilling effect spreads, it also tends to be internalized among those – especially Arab Muslims – on whom most suspicion rests. This internalization of suspicion is common in the experience of colonized peoples, too. The surveilled, the suspected, start to suspect and to doubt themselves. They produce excuses for otherwise acceptable behavior, and avoid legitimate activities and associations, that might be misconstrued. The sense of Otherness is thus reinforced.

The boundaries are blurred between different kinds of activity when "terrorism" is expanded to include aims such as "altering political, economic, or social structures." Thus not only those with the right (or wrong) "racial" or regional background come under the spotlight. Anyone not entirely content with the status quo, whether on the right or the left, consumerist or green, patriarch or feminist, has such aims, which under current legislation are effectively criminalized.

It is no surprise that the legislation created after 9/11 appeared in a world where, for example, "anti-globalization" activities had become increasingly visible and vocal, on an international level. Interestingly, early drafts of the EU "Framework Decision" on combating terrorism gave the game away. They referred to the prevention of "activities carried out by terrorist organizations to achieve their criminal aims at large international events" by informing host countries about "known terrorists" intending to attend.[31] Surely this is a reference to protesters, not "terrorists"? By eliding the differences between politics and crime, dangerous precedents are set, akin to totalitarian regimes of an Orwellian kind. As Naomi Klein says: "After September 11, politicians and pundits around the world instantly began spinning the terrorist attacks as part of a continuum of anti-American and anti-corporate violence." She gives examples of news writers who see protesters as working from "hatred of the USA" and using "intimidation" as a tactic.[32]

The chilling effect of anti-terrorist activities may thus be felt on groups directly and indirectly affected, including any dissenters from the status quo, be they members of opposition parties, protesters and dissenters, labor union members, academics, or members of religious groups critical of government policies or attitudes. These kinds of activity have not been subtle either. The American Council of Trustees and Alumni, for example, has published lists of academics who have – in their view – made unpatriotic statements.[33] One University of South Florida professor, Sami Al-Arian, was fired in the aftermath of 9/11 for comments made a decade earlier, apparently sympathetic to jihad. He was arrested, using post-9/11 expanded powers of prosecution, on February 20, 2003, on charges of supporting suicide bombings in Israel.[34] When jobs are on the line – as they are if you are a journalist or academic – it makes more risky the choice to stand out for academic or journalistic freedom.

The Orwellian dimensions of post-9/11 laws, directives, and decisions are deepest when one examines the secrecy surrounding these shifts. When suspects are "stored" off-shore, secret deportation orders issued, unannounced raids made on universities, and oblique references are made to protesters as "terrorists," the concerns of civil libertarians appear to be well founded. The chief immigration judge in America, for example, issued instructions to hundreds of judges on more than 600 "special interest" immigration cases. Michael J. Creppy wrote that "The courtroom must be closed for these cases: no visitors, no family, and no press."[35]

Withholding information on the unrefutable mosaic theory (that data may appear innocuous until fit into a bigger picture by terrorist groups) is also controversial. But it has occurred more frequently since 9/11. Secrecy is also seen in the notorious case of Jose Padilla, an American citizen arrested in Chicago and declared an enemy combatant, on suspicion that he was seeking to obtain information for building a radioactive ("dirty") bomb. He was placed in military custody, thus putting him out of reach of the courts, where no charge is required for detention, no access is allowed to a lawyer, and no presentation of evidence is necessary.

Citizens Mobilized for Surveillance

In September 2002 a group of medical students traveling
together down a Florida highway was stopped for questioning by police. The police had been tipped off by a
woman, Eunice Stone, who had overheard a conversation
in a service area diner. She claimed to have heard a
discussion of attacks and the likelihood of their success. It
convinced her that she was listening to a terrorist plot.
The young men, Kambiz Butt, Ayman Gheith, and Omer
Choudhary, were released after being held in handcuffs
for 17 hours.[36] Needless to say, if every conversation about
9/11 and its consequences were reported, the vast majority
of citizens would have been apprehended by police by
now. After 9/11, not only is everyone a potential suspect,
everyone is also a potential spy.

The ironies of this story multiply, however. For one
thing, it seems that the conversation details were fabri-
cated. The students denied having chatted about anything
remotely to do with attacks. Within a fear culture, no
doubt merely seeing "Middle Eastern" men in a Florida
diner could insinuate ideas about potential plots. But
things got worse. The hospital to which they were head-
ing, Larkin Community Hospital, Miami, then refused to
let them start the internships for which they made the
journey down Alligator Alley in the first place. As if it
were not enough to be detained for almost a day, the three
were then denied a vital part of their career training,
despite the fact that their records were entirely clean.
Having nothing to hide is no guarantee that there is
nothing to fear.[37]

Even without Middle Eastern features, of course, citizens may be vulnerable to investigation, triggered by
vigilante neighbors, managers, or colleagues. A survey

carried out in December 2002 found that 57 per cent of more than 700 American companies stated that they were willing to hand over to police agencies, but without a warrant, personal data from their consumer databases.[38] This figure has risen since 9/11. In other words, whatever the obligations and promises made to customers about confidentiality, these companies are willing to divulge data without their customers' knowledge or consent. Thus CEOs and other company officials declare themselves as combatants in the war against terrorism, joining the data-gathering effort as allied collaborators.

Recruiting such spies was a national endeavor in the summer of 2002, as the Bush administration unveiled its TIPS program ("Terrorism Information and Prevention System"). The program did not last long in its first iteration and was scaled back after popular outcry. But it was intended to include particular people who had access to people's homes – mail carriers, utilities workers, and the like – so that they could alert police to suspicious characters. In another initiative, $1.9 million in public funds was issued to boost the work of Neighborhood Watches, to train ordinary people to detect terrorist traits in the household next door or in the street. The idea was to double the number of American Neighborhood Watch groups to 15,000: "Community residents will be provided with information which will enable them to recognize signs of potential terrorist activity . . . making these residents a critical element in the detection, prevention, and disruption of terrorism."[39]

Even without these full programs in place, of course, the mobilization of ordinary citizens in the "war against terrorism" was already under way. And many in the USA have reported "suspicious" characters anyway, just because of the huge post-9/11 emphasis placed on the "enemy within" and amplified by the mass media. Similar initiatives have been announced elsewhere, too. In Australia, for instance, a national campaign was launched at the end of 2002 to warn the public of the dangers of internal terrorist strikes, following an attack that killed a number of Australian (and other) tourists in Bali, Indonesia. Like the American efforts, this is directed at ordinary citizens, who are invited to inform of any unusual behavior and report using a free hotline.[40]

One might justifiably ask why particular efforts are mounted at particular times. It could be argued, for example, that some of these "spy within" schemes have deliberately been made to coincide with political exigencies. To employ scare tactics is not unknown, and warning of "enemies within" is likely to increase anxiety that might bolster electoral support, or support for war, or support for further surveillance measures. All of these were important objectives in the summer of 2002.

Needless to say, the attempt to use ordinary citizens as surveillance operatives is not new. Yes, Neighborhood Watch schemes have grown hugely in the past few decades. But there have also been some other specific programs designed to extend policing by enlisting local aid. Indeed, during a previous "war," the "War on Drugs," there was even a precedent set in the 1970s and 1980s with the "TIPs" scheme, only at that time the letters stood for "Turn In a Pusher." With this practice in particular, "informing" took on a positive aspect as a duty expected of good citizens.[41] Frowned upon as a somewhat underhand practice in the eighteenth and nineteenth centuries, informing became a commonplace part of community policing in the later twentieth century. But as Gary T. Marx observes,[42] informers typically exaggerate what they report (no doubt to sound credible), which means that damage done to innocent reputations can be severe.

More broadly, as Onora O'Neill argued in her 2002

Reith Lectures in the UK, such activities help foster a "culture of suspicion."[43] When a panic regime is established, as has happened following 9/11, and "terrorist threats" are thought to be present everywhere, not only do all become suspects, but all are enlisted as informers. It is not only as access to numerous personal databases such as "Advance Passenger Information" for flight data or internet service provider records of emails and clickstreams is sought that suspect groups proliferate. It is also in the everyday world of ordinary people agreeing to become the "eyes and ears" of police and intelligence agencies and calling the local police station when they see or hear something "suspicious."

Intensifying Surveillance

The paradoxes and ironies of 9/11 and its aftermath will be significant features of local–global trends for some time. Extraordinary measures have been invoked in law and policy to tighten security and reduce the risks of terrorist attacks. It is as if the frequently trumpeted idea that "everything changed" on that day has become a self-fulfilling prophecy. Yet what is changing is not what was thought to have changed on 9/11. The realization that certain risks are real ones has helped to create an environment in which everything seems risky, uncertain. Even the process of plugging the security gaps seems to have the effect of raising levels of fear, rather than lowering them.

In some countries of the global north, these measures appear like a slap in the face. They are shockingly similar to tactics thought to be as "outdated" as the Cold War. And the most powerful nation on the planet is leading the way. Countries such as Australia have been quick to follow; most European ones have shown a little more caution. In others, particularly in South-East Asia, East Asia, and the Middle East, state-sponsored cultures of suspicion and secrecy are more familiar and taken-for-granted. In several of these, such as Japan and Singapore, 9/11 has been used as a pretext for continuing to pursue the same path.

Whatever they achieve as counter-terrorism, the extraordinary measures, seen for example in the American PATRIOT Act, certainly seem set to expand the culture of suspicion in the USA and elsewhere. Historical memories are short, it appears. In 1952, when the continuing need for wartime ID cards in the UK was being questioned, the judge who raised the most telling arguments said that such cards turn citizens into suspects, and the absent-minded into law-breakers. But this is exactly what is happening now, on a far larger scale and, as we shall see in the next chapter, reinforced by technologies undreamed of in the mid-twentieth century.

Secrecy deepens the difficulties. After 9/11, the culture of secrecy is spreading. Curtailing civil rights means that less is known about who is under suspicion or held in custody, or where, or why. And, as we shall see, the uses of new technology for surveillance tend to reduce further public knowledge about what is happening. Openness and transparency in communication is hard to come by post-9/11. Deliberate misinformation circulates, minimal accurate revelations are made, and that which does come out may be obscured by technological noise. Yet social trust, needed more than ever after 9/11, is actually whittled away by the low level of open communication.

Defining terrorism broadly, in ways that capture not only those genuine enemies within, but also the activities of any oppositional and dissenting groups, permits the culture of suspicion to spread even further. It serves to intensify surveillance such that no one can be sure who is to be trusted. Even the serious-minded pursuits of those who actually have the best interests of their countries at heart – wishing to preserve the environment, seek justice for the poor, the homeless, and the hungry, or to limit the power of the wealthy – are officially in doubt. Yet trust, along with respect and tolerance, is at the heart of those basic relationships that together make up the weave of the social fabric.

A sense of security is unlikely to be created by the deployment of neighbors and workmates as informers. Again, these are the very people on whom we depend from day to day. If social life is to be enjoyable and fulfilling – let alone plain possible – then these are the people whom we must trust. To say this is not to minimize for a moment the need to seek out the serious suspects who may be plotting further acts of violence and terror. But it is to argue that, if the very social fabric is not to be worn dangerously thin, the means of mutual trust and care need to be shored up, not further eroded.

3

Automating Surveillance

> To this point most of the emphasis has centered on . . .
> installing muscular sociotechnical fixes that promise
> security against terrorism and place our whole society
> under suspicion.
>
> Langdon Winner[1]

Security measures introduced since September 11
include, prominently, a number of surveillance devices
and systems. Their purpose is to increase safety and allay
fears. They are meant primarily to predict and pre-empt
danger and to restrict access to a given country or site to
eligible persons only. In other words, they are intended to
filter the fluids that flow through today's liquid societies.[2]
Once, the old sovereign power of the state was reshaped
through modern forms of discipline. But now another
shift is evident, to informational and mediated power,
seen here as surveillance. If the elusive enemy leaves only
transactional trails and communication clues, then these
can be detected by one means – automated surveillance.

The surveillance measures introduced after 9/11 are
not new. They are all devices and systems with a track
record. By and large they extend, enhance, or place in an
unfamiliar context technologies whose promise has been

advertised for some time or whose use has been proven in some other context. Biometric measures, for instance, have been tested over a number of years in several contexts, from retinal scans at bank machines to digital records of fingerprints in police databases. Now they are being deployed at airports and borders for security purposes. In the first section of this chapter I show how ailing businesses grasped at the opportunity to provide technologies for "homeland security." After 9/11 companies and government departments that already had an interest in such surveillance systems now had a rationale – and public support – for installing them.

Technologically, what these surveillance systems have in common is a reliance on searchable databases. Records can be checked and sorted at high speed according to various categories to isolate potential abnormal cases that may indicate risk. This does not hold in the case of ordinary, "live" CCTV monitoring by a human operator, for example. But it is true of the commonly advanced proposal for facial recognition facilities with CCTV. This means that they are "algorithmic," or mathematically coded for computers to make "decisions" as to what behavior, signal, word, or image fits in which category. Their key feature is thus that they are automated, dispensing as far as possible with human operatives.[3]

On one level, this chapter addresses a number of basic questions. What exactly are the surveillance systems being mounted and reinforced in response to 9/11? Which devices are being promoted (and by whom) as the keys to security? What does this mean in terms of the already existing developments in surveillance at the turn of the twenty-first century? What do they mean in a larger, longer-term frame? And what are the likely consequences of installing these systems in what appears to be a new global alliance of surveillance states?

Beyond this, the chapter revolves around a number of critical issues. Automating surveillance will not solve all problems at a (key)stroke. Indeed, many problems are themselves caused by automating surveillance. Unfortunately, most systems retain embarrassing limitations and flaws as far as their overt rationale is concerned. There are also several unintended consequences of automating surveillance that deserve attention.

First, the question of strategy. Terrorism today appropriates successfully a network style of organization that may be emerging as the dominant mode, at least in the global north.[4] But does the new surveillance match this? It is not clear that asymmetric, mobile, and networked power will be thwarted by top-down, integrated surveillance.

Second, the technical questions. At a simple level, we cannot rest assured that, technically, some of the systems devised, promoted, or installed will actually work, at least in the ways that their champions claim. Many systems were already in place before 9/11 that did nothing to prevent the original attacks.

Third, the unintended consequences. Extensive social "collateral damage" will be inflicted using the new methods. Automated surveillance is essentially a means of social sorting, of trying to assess in advance who is a suspect. That it cannot easily achieve this aim does not mean that nothing will result. Automated surveillance simply places yet more people under suspicion. The surveillance web[5] is being widened and ordinary people in their everyday lives will be exposed to more monitoring.

Fourth, the roads not taken. By comparison with high-technology surveillance solutions, little is heard about non- or low-technological approaches. On the one hand, this might include old-fashioned undercover intelligence gathering. On the other, there appear to be few resources devoted to attempting to understand and address the underlying causes of twenty-first-century terrorism.

Automating surveillance represents a continuation, albeit at an accelerated pace, of trends that were already strongly present in all advanced industrial societies. "Surveillance society" describes well the personal and population data-processing aspect of the "knowledge-based" or "information society." It is the necessary obverse of the coin of distributed production and of doing things at a distance. All interactions and transactions are monitored to increase efficiency and speed.[6] One trend is accented, however: an unprecedented convergence between state and commercial surveillance, and this is the main theme of chapter 4.

Placed in a larger perspective, these trends also show that after 9/11 "technology" is still seen as a savior, as a first resort. Technological fixes are the common currency of crisis in late modern societies. This is nothing new either, but the quest for technologies, geared to guaranteed security, has been gathering pace especially since the Second World War. Indeed, DARPA policies helped guide large-scale leading-edge computer development from the 1960s.[7] Technological solutions are invoked before other more labor-intensive and human-oriented surveillance methods (which, ironically, are in fact more likely to succeed), let alone efforts aimed at mutual understanding and the reduction of western threats to Middle Eastern countries that spawn Islamism.

Selling Surveillance

Security and surveillance devices have emerged as an increasingly important market segment in the past decades, and selling surveillance is highly significant today.[8]

True, sales were slipping before 9/11, but the aftermath of the attacks offered new hope. A big burst of business activity occurred in the high-tech sector immediately after 9/11, especially in the USA. High-ranking technology leaders from companies such as Hewlett-Packard, AOL-Time-Warner, and AT&T flew to Washington DC to meet with administration officials in the weeks following the attacks. How could American high technology, including Silicon Valley, aid in the "war against terrorism"?[9]

Government attention was welcome, even if Silicon Valley companies were not used to selling to government. The shift did not occur overnight, of course. Although a dramatic upsurge of business interest in security issues occurred in the months just after 9/11[10] the real take-off took some while to occur. The slowness of movement is probably due to several factors: the earlier buoyancy of the private sector, the distance between the west and east coast of the USA, and, perhaps most significantly, the bureaucratic hurdles to rapid decision-making in the public sector. Companies also hesitated to make immediate decisions to create internal positions to oversee the shift from commercial to "homeland security" operations.[11] Although not-for-profit proposals have also been made through the National Research Council[12], the main focus has been on companies that sell security and surveillance devices for profit.

It is clear from the business pages that companies jockeyed to position themselves for procurements, not least because information technology sales had been lagging for some time prior to 9/11. Interest in surveillance technologies was good news for companies in the doldrums of an economic slump. Only one or two companies – such as InVision Technologies Inc., and the Lockheed-Martin Corporation – have actually seen their share values rise appreciably since 9/11, however.[13] This despite the biggest single procurement at the time of writing being to Unisys, who hold a three year contract worth US$3 billion to build the technology infrastructure for the Transportation Security Administration, the new airport security agency.[14] But the other companies could afford to wait.

Funds were made available. The Bush Administration earmarked US$38 billion in new spending for homeland security in the federal fiscal year 2003. Companies have been quick to try to obtain their share. The CIA, for example, through its venture arm "In-Q-Tel," is funding many company projects. They deal – despite the James Bond "Q" tag – in mundane-sounding Internet search services, data organization software, security and privacy technology, and virtual 3D products.[15] Dynago Inc. produces competitive and market intelligence for companies, scouring web pages for revealing patterns of words. The FBI can use this technology for examining documents created by suspected terrorists. Khojna Technologies checks documents of public companies for regulatory agencies, and this can be turned to scrutinizing financial records of those who may be funding terrorism. Sightech Inc., which works with moving pattern recognition – pop bottles on an assembly line with badly fitting caps will be noticed, for instance – has spun off a new branch, "IntelliVision." Similar software can spot a passenger who leaves a bag on a concourse.[16] The list goes on.

Some surveillance technologies were already flourishing in the market place; others were retooled from commercial to security purposes. Either way, 9/11 was seen as an economic opportunity to be exploited, in order to get out of the existing slump. As one commercial businessman turned In-Q-Tel CEO put it, "All you could really say before is that we made a lot of money." Now, "You can say we're really doing something for the public good."[17] But whatever the altruistic rationale, an economic factor is deeply implicated in the technology-versus-terrorism drive. While this factor has to be considered alongside others, which together explain the rapid rise of technological surveillance, it is a mistake to minimize its significance.

Surveillance Technologies

Four main means of improving technological surveillance have been proposed since 9/11. They are:

- biometrics, the use of data extracted from the body, such as an iris scan, digital image, or fingerprint;
- identification (ID) cards with embedded programmable chips ("smart cards");
- Closed Circuit Television (CCTV), or video surveillance, often enhanced by facial recognition software;
- communicational measures, such as wiretaps and other message interception methods including Web-based surveillance.

In some places, several of these measures are now in place, while others had to await legal change and are now being implemented. These are overlapping, specific techniques. In the next chapter, the integration of systems is investigated.

Biometrics has to do with the verification of identities, on the assumption that truly unique identifiers are found in the body. These may be used in smart cards, and are implicated in CCTV facial recognition systems as well. Smart cards, similarly, are intended to ensure a one-to-one fit between the identity of the card-holder and the unique card and thus to prevent unauthorized use or access. CCTV systems may be used "live" to monitor persons in transit for risky behaviors (for example at airports) but also may be enhanced using databases of facial images or other biometrics such as retinal scans. Communicational surveillance is intended to check for potentially dangerous messages passing between suspect persons and groups.

Communicational surveillance is concerned primarily with *monitoring* behaviors, as is "live" CCTV. All the others, including facial recognition, are more concerned with *identifying* individuals. But these two are linked. The Echelon system of international intelligence monitors *in order to* identify messages, and their senders, that seem risky.[18] Surprise was expressed after 9/11 that the monitoring technologies did not seem to have provided warnings (although it now appeared, rather, that the warnings given were not heeded in a coordinated fashion).[19] As we shall see, the trend is toward the use of more identifying technologies, and this has important consequences. Communicational surveillance is more fully discussed in chapter 5.

Each of these surveillance technologies, or clusters of technologies, has some bearing on the garnering of personal data. The massive system known as Total Information Awareness (TIA), a vast electronic net designed to detect suspicious behavior patterns, is not unrelated to the surveillance enhancements discussed here. However, it deserves some comment in its own right, and is discussed in the context of converging and integrating surveillance (in chapter 4). It must be noted that many other kinds of system are also being upgraded or established following 9/11 as adjuncts to these technologies. Securing remote access to corporate networks, creating firewalls and intrusion-detection systems, installing messaging and mobile wireless systems to connect law enforcement agencies, police and fire departments are all examples of this. But as our main focus is on surveillance, it is surveillance technologies that are the prime focus here. Each system, or system-cluster, is examined in turn.

Biometrics

Recent advances in biometrics have made the use of physical attributes – body parts, if you will – popular candidates for identification systems. Some means are sought of verifying claims to identity and privilege, and unique physical attributes such as fingerprints, irises, retinas, hand geometry, vein patterns, voices, and faces are good tokens. Of course, these are never fully permanent tokens, so one can only ever claim a "probable" match. Such systems are most reliable when used in conjunction with others. If someone makes a claim at a bank with a name, and that is supported by a biometric identifier, the probability of error is low. Errors are much more likely when the system has to identify an individual on its own.

The system must acquire an image, using an appropriate scanner, before localizing it for processing. The image must be cleaned by removing extraneous information, and the remaining minutiae turned into a template for eventual comparison with attributes stored in the database. The "minutiae" are the uniquely distinguishing features of the image. They include the whorl on the fingerprint or the mole on the face scan for which matches are then sought on the database. Of course, DNA is reliable in this context, too. But because it is invasive and requires special expertise, it is unlikely to be used for more than forensic purposes in the near future. The others have been seeking mass market acceptance for the past few years.

Biometrics, then, is a more general term than the others, and indeed may be implicated in ID cards or

CCTV systems. Biometrics relies on having access to some physical characteristic, and then on algorithms that enable the verification process to be automated. An example is iris scanners, installed at Schiphol Airport in Amsterdam in October 2001.[20] The "Privium" system is intended to fast-track passengers carrying the iris data-embedded smart card – this is a voluntary system, of course – through passport control and customs. This system does not use a database; the scanner simply checks the eyes to see if they match the ones recorded on the card. In 2003 the Dutch government plans to seal the bearer's iris code into passports.[21] In Canada, before 9/11, iris scans were mainly associated with bank machine tests.[22]

Another example is provided by "Smartgate," currently in the trial stage at Sydney airport in Australia. This replaces the face-to-passport check normally done by a Customs official, with an automated operation. Passengers place passports on a scanner, watched by a camera that takes less than 10 seconds to verify identity. The machine takes into account age, ethnicity, as well as expression and changes such as hairstyle and glasses.[23]

Other systems use, or in the case of Canada plan to use, fingerprint scanners to enhance security. Canadian airports, ship-ports, and border crossings will have equipment linked to FBI and RCMP (Royal Canadian Mounted Police) databases, to identify terrorists whose fingerprints are on file.[24] While international airline authorities have applauded the relatively reliable eye-based scanners, Japanese researcher Tsutomu Matsumoto recently tested several fingerprint scanners, fooling them with his gelatin-based fake finger. He also lifted latent prints from glass and used his photoshop to enhance them to make yet more "fingers."[25]

ID Cards

Immediately after the 9/11 attacks, with almost indecent alacrity, Larry Ellison, president of the Silicon Valley's Oracle – the largest American database software company – offered the US government free smart card software for a national ID system.[26] What a commercial coup that would have been had his offer been accepted! There was no mention at the time, of course, of what price would be charged for each access to the Oracle database, or the roll-out price-tag on a national smart card identifier. Such cards are increasingly popular among businesses, and are seen by many as an obvious means of upgrading identification systems in the war against terrorism. In their more reliable versions they depend on biometrics.

Various kinds of biometric identifiers may be used to authenticate ID cards. The government of Peru, for example, issues photo ID cards with an embedded face-recognition chip for residents.[27] DNA patterns have been proposed for ID cards in the USA,[28] and, so the pundits say, ID implants are also likely to be marketed soon.[29] Because of the body-invasive nature of implants, it is fair to assume that these could only be administered in situations of extreme authoritarian control. It is clear, however, that since 9/11 "smart" ID cards have been consistently touted as a key means of enhancing security. They represent a way of being sure that people are who they say they are and that they have a right or a reason to be where they are.

Other "crises" have sparked similar calls for new ID card systems over the past few decades. During the twentieth century, world wars were a major impetus to the widespread and routine use of identification documents. In some countries these remained in place after the war was over; in others, such as the UK, the ID card system was dismantled following the scaling down of the "warfare state" – if only to be replaced by the ID documents that accompanied the welfare state.[30] Calls for ID cards were repeated during the worst IRA attacks in the UK in the mid-1990s, and soon afterwards in Spain, in response to the ETA (Basque separatist) attacks.

It is highly likely that several of the schemes proposed after 9/11 will be implemented, though not necessarily in the original form proposed. There is little doubt, for example, that Larry Ellison's offer was serious or that Oracle could have backed it up. The idea of using "smart" cards on a very large scale for ID purposes has been projected in commercial and administrative schemes for several years, not least because it represents a technological "next step" from less complex and comprehensive systems. Multipurpose commercial smart cards (such as Mondex[31]) were tested during the 1990s. And some countries, such as Malaysia, Thailand, and Hong Kong, have already started to implement similar cards as national IDs. But others, such as the USA, the UK, and Canada, have held back – or at least they did until September 11, 2001.

The apparent threat of terrorism to national security helped to put electronic ID cards back on national agendas. Several proposals were made in the aftermath of the September 11 attacks, no doubt to test the waters of public opinion. While Larry Ellison's offer was turned down, the US nevertheless embarked on a process that could well culminate in the use of enhanced drivers' license cards (and their surrogates) acting as national IDs. Although part of the justification for these schemes is the knowledge that several of the 19 highjackers of September 11 were using assumed IDs, it is not clear that the American public will agree to universal identifiers. Opinion polls show a declining acceptance of such schemes, and, in particular, doubt about the competence of drivers' license authorities to have charge of them.

Other countries, such as Germany and the UK, have also looked at new national ID systems in order to strengthen security in the wake of September 11. The British "entitlement card" is being phased in as a smart card with biometrics identifiers, building on the already introduced "Applicant Registration Cards," which are designed to help cope with asylum seekers. Although it is officially denied that the Entitlement Card is an anti-terrorist measure as such, the chances of its being at least indirectly used for such purposes are strong. In the German case, machine-readable cards introduced after a political tussle in 1987 will be upgraded using hologram technology. Yet other countries, such as Malaysia and Spain, have claimed that the systems that were already being implemented in those countries will have the effect of reducing terrorist threats. Countries are also looking to each other to provide models, guidance, or warnings about potential failure, abuse, or other unintended consequences.[32]

In South-East Asia, both Malaysia and Hong Kong are in the process of introducing national smart card IDs. This follows Thailand's adoption of a Sun Microsystems ID backbone within its National Registration System. Malaysia's "Mykad" is currently optional, and contains a driver's license and passport information. In Europe, Spain is introducing a national smart card ID as well, partly in an attempt to demonstrate its leadership in European high-technology developments. In each of these cases, change was well under way before September 11. These initiatives are not unopposed, however. In the early months of 2002, for instance, considerable controversy was evident in Hong Kong over the new capabilities of the smart card, designed primarily to reduce illegal Chinese immigration.

In countries such as France, Japan, and Canada, much interest has been shown in the possibility of introducing new ID systems, including the use of smart card technologies. If adopted, they are likely to be built onto existing systems. In Canada, for example, since 2001 public hearings have been held in Quebec regarding the Telehealth smart card project, which, if implemented as planned, will have several features. The cards confirm admissibility to services, create statements of services used by patients, produce data on insured services, give access to a provincial patient index, and so on. Such a system would offer useful lessons for smart card use and acceptability. And in a federal program, new immigrants are now issued with a "Permanent Resident" photo ID card with biometrics measures, a move prompted by the attacks of September 2001.

There are several difficulties with the new ID cards, however. For one thing, they are usually only as reliable as the other documents they are based on. This is often, ultimately, the birth certificate, a document that is notoriously easy to falsify if one has a mind to do it.[33] In Canada, as a response to 9/11, proposals are now being made to upgrade all birth certificates issued prior to 1984, to permit electronic cross-checking.[34] Secondly, if central databases are used, these become very vulnerable to attack. But thirdly, assuming these problems are overcome, there is still the difficulty that, to put it simply, suicide bombers do not strike twice. It is unlikely that the kinds of terrorist to whom the ID cards are an answer will ever find their way onto suspect lists.

On another level, it has to be said that the new generation of smart ID cards has, even more prominently than in earlier systems, the task of classifying and discriminating between different groups of person. They are intended to check for illegal immigrants or other persons in transit who have inadequate documentation. This is obvious to any observer, but what may be less than obvious is the negatively discriminatory practices that can easily accompany the use of such identifiers. The history of the twentieth century is replete with such regrettable practices. Obvious cases were Hitler's Germany, South Africa under apartheid, Rwanda during the genocide years, and contemporary Israel;[35] but others might include countries such as the USA and Canada, where persons of Japanese origin (using the census for ID) were mistreated during the Second World War. Even now, following 9/11, there is evidence that some Arab and Muslim people in the USA have been singled out for very negative treatment, including lengthy detention without charge or trial.[36]

CCTV and Face-recognition

When the word "surveillance" comes up in conversation, it is often video surveillance, or CCTV, that people have in mind. Video surveillance seems to be both a cause and effect of scopophilia, and appears to be a very twenty-first-century phenomenon that engenders both fear and fascination. Yet its popularity as a means of surveillance is rooted in some twentieth-century trends in social control, and its efficacy in achieving goals of crime prevention is often exaggerated. The "twenty-first-century" features are seen in the effort to make CCTV "intelligent" by switching from human operators to automated systems of movement and face-recognition.

Biometrics is implicated in new generation CCTV systems, where face-recognition is involved. Some airports, including Pearson International in Toronto, already had limited systems used in conjunction with a search of suspects already in place. Keflavik Airport in Iceland announced in September 2001 that all visitors' faces would be screened. During October 2001 American airports were quick to respond with news that face-recognition technology would be installed. Oakland International laid claim to being first in the USA, using the system to check on passengers detained under suspicion (policing authorities determine who they are), but a much broader system was announced at Boston Logan Airport.[37] This uses Visionics "FaceIt" technology at an undisclosed checkpoint to compare facial characteristics of all travelers, airport employees, and flight crews with those of suspected terrorists.[38]

In this field, airport security is most closely associated with urban CCTV systems. An ordinary crowd of Superbowl fans in Tampa Florida was scanned using Viisage equipment in January 2001 (and amongst the 100,000 people scanned about 19 petty criminals were recognized). Similar equipment has been used for some time in the 300 cameras on public streets in the Newham district of east London, UK. This was mainly in response to the IRA threats of the 1990s, but street camera systems in the UK got their biggest single boost from the 1993 James Bulger case, involving the toddler murdered by young boys who were caught on camera.[39] Britain is easily the world leader in using CCTV in public places, but the face-recognition aspect is only present in some very limited sites. It is unclear whether face-recognition systems work for cases of street crime in public places (despite the claims of their promoters), let alone whether their limited successes there can be re-applied to cases of international terrorism.[40]

There was mounting pressure before 9/11 to develop and to install face-recognition CCTV systems.[41] This came, for instance, from the US Defense Department as well as from a number of major companies and think-tanks such as the Rand Organization. The Defense Advanced Research Projects Agency (DARPA) had anti-terrorism in mind, but private corporations sought customers from banks, motor vehicle officials, and others. Imagis, a Vancouver-based company, vigorously promoted its products before and after 9/11. They sell to casinos, and also to the RCMP (the Pearson airport system) and the FBI. They market their software through Groupe Bull in France, and Fujitsu and NTT in Japan. The Peruvian ID system is also based on Imagis technology.[42]

While many promises are made for face-recognition CCTV, the reality is that, like the other biometric technologies, it has only limited uses and reliability. Some airports use it to scan airport employees, such as maintenance workers and baggage handlers. When there is a known database for employee identification, the two checks (biometric and ID) can work together satisfactorily. But picking terrorists out of crowds is a quite different issue. The question is, "does this biometric match anyone in the crowd?"[43] – but terrorists do not pose for photos (and are likely to use evasive techniques and disguises). And even if one had some good images, the so-called base-rate fallacy means that the chances of false alarms are very high indeed (9,999 for one terrorist – which means a full alert each time).

It is also argued that face-recognition systems, while they may not work for their ostensible purposes, would end up being used for finding petty criminals. These people will already have their image in the database, and will thus stand more chance of being "seen" by the camera. But there are further arguments raised against face-recognition. The potential for abuse – such as tracking individuals – is huge. And data is easily combined with that from other systems such as tracing systems of the E-911 (locatable emergency telephone call) type. There could also be "premature disclosure," as Philip Agre calls it, similar to that offered by call display telephones, but based on the passing face-image. Informed and meaningful consent is almost impossible to obtain, and the chances are also high that civil liberties will be overridden in places where systems are established, especially if there is a weak tradition of appeal to them.[44]

Technological Surveillance after 9/11

Technological surveillance responses to September 11 have proliferated. High-tech companies, waiting in the wings for the opportunity to launch their products, saw September 11 providing just the platform they needed. Not surprisingly, given the haste to find solutions, and the apparent lack of independent research that would assess technology claims, almost all the "experts" on whom the media call for comment are representatives of companies. Thus, for instance, Michael G. Cherkasky, president of a security firm, Kroll, suggested that "every American could be given a 'smart card' so, as they go into an airport or anywhere, we know exactly who they are."[45] Ellison's offer had a similar rationale behind it.

As we have seen, many other technical surveillance-related responses to September 11 have appeared: iris-scanners are installed at airports, for example, Schiphol, Amsterdam, elsewhere in Europe, and in parts of North America. CCTV cameras proliferate in public places, enhanced if possible with facial-recognition capacities such as the Mandrake system in Newham, south London. Systems based on genetic data are also proposed, plus far-reaching forms of communications interception (discussed in chapter 5). Each of these systems is proposed as a means of making "the world a safer place." But the evidence reviewed here does not necessarily support such sanguine hopes. It cannot easily be shown that they work with the kind of precision that is required. So they may not achieve the ends intended.

Secondly, not only are the claims made for the new technologies dubious, they also have considerable potential for negative social consequences.[46] There is a lamentable lack of informed comment on these far-reaching developments, particularly in the USA, where the most advanced systems are being proposed and promoted. The new technologies are likely to have unintended consequences that include privacy invasion, gratuitous limitations on freedom of movement, and the reinforcing of forms of social division and exclusion within the countries where they are established.

A third and larger dimension of the technological aspect of surveillance practices is that seeking superior technologies appears as a primary goal. No matter that the 9/11 "terrorism" involved reliance on relatively aged technologies – jet aircraft of a type that have been around for 30 years, sharp knives, and so on – it is assumed that high-tech solutions are called for. Moreover, the kinds of technology sought – iris scans, face-recognition, smart cards, biometrics, DNA – rely heavily on the use of searchable databases, with the aim of anticipating, preempting, and preventing acts of "terrorism" by isolating in advance potential perpetrators.

A key effect of 9/11 is to bring the apparatus and the assemblage into closer coordination with each other.[47] As we have seen, the rhizomic operation of consumer surveillance can be raided by police and intelligence services, when required to do so. This fourth theme is elaborated in chapter 4, so I shall not anticipate it here.

The effect of increased automated, algorithmic surveillance is, fifthly, to deepen the process of social sorting, of categorization for various purposes. It is a means of inclusion and exclusion, of acceptance and rejection, of worthiness and unworthiness. What may be called "digital discrimination" consists of the ways in which the flows of personal data – abstracted information – are sifted and channeled in the process of risk assessment, to privilege some and disadvantage others, to accept some as legitimately present and to reject others. Note also that this is increasingly done *in advance* of any offence. Automated surveillance is frequently pre-emptive, reminiscent of the "Pre-Crime Department" in Spielberg's 2002 movie *Minority Report*, which intercepted murderers before they struck.[48]

The longer-term consequences of this are as yet uncertain. But one thing is becoming clear: although privacy laws and data-protection are very important, by themselves they remain inadequate as a means of limiting today's newly augmented surveillance power. Indeed, privacy and data-protection laws were introduced only to limit the *uses* to which data are put, not to limit data collection itself. There is a significant "care" motif[49] in the post-9/11 measures, in that they are introduced to enhance security. Yet the balance seems to be tipping precipitately in favor of heightened "control" in which general surveillance spreads to the population at large. This is neither inevitable nor irrevocable. It is a trend which, if unchecked, could become a serious threat to human rights. The language of privacy is, indeed, of decreasing salience to the emerging situation of rhizomic, algorithmic, assemblage-type surveillance.[50] But this does not mean either that some notions lying behind privacy concerns are irrelevant, or that a fresh vocabulary for mobilizing dissent is superfluous. On the contrary, without it, some very regressive tendencies that have become apparent since 9/11 will simply be reinforced.

Consequences and Critique

One need have no quarrel with the idea that serious measures should be taken to prevent repetition of the horrendous events of September 11, 2001. What such measures might include is a good question. It is easy to fall in with the agendas of those who wish merely to shore up defenses, rather than exploring the possibilities for change in the global north. Much scope exists for reducing the threat of an oil-dependent "western way of life" to Arab countries, among others.

In the context of this chapter, however, it must be stressed that merely technological solutions are in themselves not only inadequate to the threat, but also dangerous to democratic polity. They are dangerous because of three key trends, illustrated in the foregoing discussion:

- the effective recentralization of state power;
- the increased capacity to discriminate between different classes of person – dubiously categorized – using algorithmic surveillance;
- the relative lack of accountability of these systems, paralleled by the willingness of populations to accept them as the "price of security."

As we shall see in the next chapter, the convergence and integration of surveillance systems complicates and compounds these matters all the more.

The problem with the last point, about security, is of course that the intended consequences of the technologies considered here are unlikely to be realized. Studying these various deployments and proposals brings a deep sense of futility. On the one hand, integrated and hierarchical systems are poor means for resisting networked, mobile, asymmetric powers of contemporary terrorism. On the other, the evidence from specific devices such as biometrics, ID cards, facial-recognition associated with CCTV, and communications monitoring is that as tools for an anti-terrorist campaign they are flawed. Automated, algorithmic systems are poorly equipped, by and large, for the task of identifying or monitoring the actions or messages of previously unknown potential terrorists. Moreover, to the extent that surveillance depends on information technologies, the easier it will be for persons who wish to evade detection to do so, just because human beings are more flexible and imaginative than technologies. Any technology can be outwitted, given time and ingenuity.

Many unintended consequences follow from the tightening of security by surveillance. There is already closer monitoring of all who are in fact "clean" (and have a data image to prove it). The culture of control will colonize more areas of life, with our permission or without. This is because of what Mike Davis calls the "globalization of fear,"[51] which propels politicians into premature policies. Add to this the understandable desire for security, combined with the pressure to adopt particular kinds of systems, and the results are almost predictable. Ordinary citizens, workers, and consumers – that is, people with no terrorist ambitions whatsoever – find that their life-chances are more circumscribed by the categories into which they fall. For some, those categories are particularly prejudicial. They already restrict them from consumer choices because of credit ratings, or, more insidiously, relegate them to second-class status because of their color or ethnic background. Now, there is an added category to fear: the terrorist. It's an old story in high-tech guise.

The alternatives to high-tech monitoring and identification methods seem to receive little attention. Labor-intensive intelligence gathering, physical checking at airports, the use of security personnel to screen travelers – these all have an apparently low premium compared with the extension of surveillance systems with a new biometric or search device. Yet if one examines reports of the discovery and arrest of suspected terrorist groups in Europe and elsewhere, the means involve little or no high technology. The infiltration of likely groups, the use of reliable informers, and the casual talk of undercover and plainclothes agents are the items that seem to produce results. The 26-year-old Jordanian Shadi Abdullah is a case in point. Arrested in Krefeld, Germany, in April 2002, he provided intelligence authorities with a wealth of information on Qaeda operations in Europe and other countries.[52]

Actually mounting programs to try to understand the reasons why certain countries, religious adherents, or political groups would have serious enough misgivings about and mistrust of the western world to sacrifice their lives in order to destroy it seems well beyond the pale. This is not only labor-intensive, it would also involve slow learning processes and cultural contacts of apparently very unwelcome kinds.[53]

Much better, it appears, to fall back on the technological fix, just as has been done for over 30 years, since the first highjackings prompted technical modifications to aircraft and airport facilities. There is tremendous commercial pressure to purchase new surveillance equipment. The current situation is seen as an unprecedented business opportunity by some who have seen their share prices rise several-fold since 9/11. American security companies in particular are hawking their wares around the world in the hope of taking advantage of the political climate of anti-terrorist activity.

CEOs such as Larry Ellison are still arguing that the interests of Oracle and the USA are virtually identical and that they lie in integrated ID systems.[54]

In the absence of other positive proposals, the automated solutions will no doubt continue to appear attractive. The persistence of faith in high technology even in the face of its published shortcomings is not a novel phenomenon. In the context of drug-testing techniques, for example, Elaine Draper speaks of a "lemming effect" in which, when "one company adopts drug testing other companies rush to follow it, even without strong evidence that tests are scientifically defensible."[55] There is surely more here than mere confidence in one's products, or even the products of others. The underlying motif is what David Noble calls the "religion of technology."[56] This is a set of implicit commitments, common in western societies, which bind us to continuing the technical quest but blind us to its limitations. Like other religious ideas, these ones tend to vary in emphasis over time. Today's electronic epiphanies, suggests Paul Virilio, invoke "ubiquity, instantaneity, and immediacy" – characteristics that are certainly sought in new surveillance technologies.[57]

Political (and public) fears continue to produce emergency regimes, reminiscent, but on a larger scale, of earlier moral panics.[58] Safety and security are good things to desire, but the means are highly dubious, and spring from other sources. So why the fixation on technology?[59] I suggest that this is articulated with one of the deepest currents of (late) modernity: the deep-seated belief in the power of technology to protect and to guarantee progress. Jacques Ellul's concept of *la technique,* a relentless cultural commitment to technological progress via ever-augmented means, finds strong echoes today.[60] This represents the derailing of the worthy belief that carefully crafted technology may contribute to human betterment.

None of the foregoing supports the idea that technological applications are simply inappropriate weapons in the war against terrorism. Rather, several questions about the proposed systems have not been asked, or, if they have, the questions have not been heard. The problem is that some questions are very big ones. Will the solutions speak to the networking strategy of today's terrorism? Are the systems capable of producing the promised goods? What of the unintended consequences, including those that may already be seen from the operation of other systems? Nor can much encouragement be gained from assuming that the technologies will not do all that is claimed for them. While this is true, civil rights and social trust are not positively protected by technical ineptitude.

And indeed, much is claimed for the technologies. Too much. It is not merely that the large-scale systems under construction are likely to fail badly (a "good" failure, suggests Bruce Schneier, is slow, delaying an attack[61]) but that to debate security and surveillance in merely technological terms is myopic to say the least. This is not the place to argue the point, but attempts to produce security by using surveillance technologies tend to insist on a particular form of argument, which then invites counter-argument along the same narrowly technical lines. Important though the technical arguments are, focusing on these alone creates a dangerous impasse. Automating surveillance sounds, correctly, as if people are less and less involved in the process. As I have suggested, this is a dangerous trend. Not only should people be involved in every stage of each security-related initiative, but a larger context of communication is also required. In that larger context, dialogue rather than (technical) monologues are sought, as a means of inspiring social trust, and of addressing not only the effects of terrorism, but also its causes.

It does no good simply to complain about technologies. In the modern world we have created situations of radical dependence on high technology that are now very hard to reverse. But some courses can be changed, and they will have to be changed by a new breed of technological citizens. By this, I do not mean citizens who are engineers and software designers, although they should not be absent either. Rather, I mean ordinary citizens who take responsibility for technological decisions at a local level (which inevitably affects the global). Our radical dependence on technology makes contemporary societies very vulnerable not only to attack but also to breakdown. If what I have argued above is correct, then simply seeking technological solutions to attacks may make freedom itself more fragile. There has to be another way: technology won't save us – not even automated surveillance.

4

Integrating Surveillance

> The key to fighting terrorism is information. Elements of the solution include gathering a much broader array of data than we do currently.
>
> DARPA[1]

Some rather telling TV images circulated after September 11. They depicted Mohammed Atta, the alleged leader of the 9/11 conspirators, in the days leading up to the attacks. He could be seen on grainy CCTV film footage entering a motel, paying for fuel at a gas station, picking up supplies in a convenience store, and so on. Not only were there images; his transactional data had been retrieved, showing his online air ticket purchase, his phone calls, his email use. Each detail was logged by airlines, phone companies and service providers. His trail was easy to follow, after the event, and yielded quite a detailed picture of his activities, and those of his colleagues.

These items did not initially form a police record or an intelligence report. They are merely the electronic footprints left by an (extra)ordinary consumer, a trail of transactions. They are unremarkable, taken-for-granted aspects of everyday life in a world of credit cards, bank machines, and the Internet. What is striking about them is how quickly the authorities were able to pull the bits of consumer data together, to construct a jigsaw of pieces which, when assembled, made up a partial portrait. Although policing and intelligence have always relied on such snippets and fragments of ordinary life activities, the crucial factor today is that they are so readily and instantly available.

This instant availability of multifarious personal data also lies behind the US "Total Information Awareness" initiative that originated in the Pentagon. Although at the time of writing it had received a political setback,[2] and may not be completed in its full form, its attractiveness to persons with a background in military intelligence (the initiative comes from DARPA, and is in the hands of John Poindexter) is clear. It offers vast resources to root out the "enemy within." It is a data-mining program, based on similar ones in the consumer realm, designed to identify terrorists and to anticipate their activities. But the data being mined is hauled up electronic shafts from familiar veins of everyday life transactions – relating to credit, travel, telephone, internet, and email. Similar features characterize at least two other major post-9/11 schemes: CAPPS II (the airline passenger screening system described in the next chapter) and the integrated driver's license identification system (mentioned in the previous one).

The convergence and integration of very different kinds of surveillance – police, intelligence, and consumer – deserves to be explored in its own right. Paradoxically, while this convergence depends heavily on the advent and the widespread adoption of searchable databases, it can in no sense be reduced to a technical level. Such computer systems are used to enable surveillance of both the highly coercive, policing variety, and also the more commercial, marketing strategies of big corporations. But the systems themselves are socially shaped by economic, political, and cultural forces that also grant them their opportunity and determine the ways they will be utilized. The one system should not be confused with the other, yet they do have some significant features in common. The social logic of marketing is different from that of policing in some important respects. But both depend on networked computer systems and stored, searchable records. And both contribute to contemporary modes of governance and social ordering in ways that are mutually reinforcing.

This chapter examines the integration of previously separate surveillance systems. This means that the social causes and consequences of convergence have to be sought. Surveillance cannot be explained in purely technical terms, even when high-tech automated systems are in question. And nor can it be understood properly by focusing only on the range of techniques discussed in chapter 3. How these are linked together in an increasingly seamless web is also highly significant.

The 9/11 attacks draw attention to some crucial features of governance that were already emerging, not only before the attacks, but before the advent of remotely searchable databases on which today's automated surveillance depends. Such forms of governance are based on risk management, and on a shift away from some kinds of social discipline towards greater control-at-a-distance. They are integrally related to the economic restructuring of the last third of the twentieth century, with its deregulation of markets, its fostering of globalization, and its focus on communication and information technologies. It is the last item that yields the means for automated and converging surveillance, but this tail does not wag the dog.

Total Information Awareness

The new Department of Homeland Security funded the development of the Pentagon's brainchild, the Total Information Awareness (TIA) Office in 2002. The initial cost was US $62.9 million; the program will cost US$245 million in 2001–3.[3] Its mission, if finally approved, is to "detect, classify, and identify foreign terrorists – and decipher their plans – and thereby enable the US to take timely action to successfully preempt and defeat terrorist acts."[4] It involves building a very large-scale counter-terrorism database that will "invent new algorithms for mining, combining, and refining data." Most of the data is of the kind that database marketers have been sifting through for a number of years in order to profile customers singled out for special "relationships," but this is the first time that a government agency has attempted to do the same for other purposes.

This illustrates perfectly the idea of "integrating surveillance." Intelligence, apart from at the height of the Cold War, is normally thought to involve external enemies, whereas policing is generally assumed to relate to domestic populations. But techniques for gathering data on foreign spies and subversives are now to be used internally. Equally, one might once have thought that, apart from fully warranted cases of police suspicion, ordinary consumer records would be of no interest to anyone but marketers. Today, the TIA program is being constructed to sidestep those old boundaries, and to delve into everyday details such as bank machine purchases, credit card receipts, Web cookies, school transcripts, medical files, magazine and newspaper subscriptions, airline manifests, property deeds, and of course addresses and telephone numbers.

Data-mining of this type usually occurs in marketing operations. Customer Relationship Management (CRM) updates electronically the old idea that the salesperson does best when the customer is known individually or, if possible, personally. It analyzes past transactions, statements of preference found on warranty forms, and, for those buying online, information about surfing and purchases captured from web server logs. Then CRM analyzes this data, profiling people by using warehousing, mining, and other complex software-driven techniques, to segment consumers into groups based on the profiles. In so doing, of course, it evacuates the relationship of anything remotely personal, but it does give marketers the means of discriminating between consumers and choosing to target for special treatment those worth most to the firm.

It takes little imagination to see how these techniques may be applied to the search for terrorists (however broadly defined), for example by creating data-mining profiles of people trying to gain access to web-based government information. In the consumer sphere, it is clear that few really know how their personal data is being used. The kind of respect that might be accorded to a customer encountered face-to-face is absent. Generally the customer does not even know the data is being stored, let along processed for profiling purposes. According to one study, "the public is concerned, indeed often outraged, when they discover the ways in which they are graded, sorted, and excluded from opportunities that others enjoy."[5] How much more might people react negatively when they discover the ways in which their personal consumer data is being used to sort them into categories of risk as potential terrorists?

However, in December 2002 it was clear that DARPA had given little or no thought to these kinds of question.

The Electronic Privacy Information Center (EPIC) filed a Freedom of Information request that the military release any review of the privacy implications of TIA, and the response was a report that had been issued in 2001 before the TIA program had been announced.[6] This report was the result of an annual meeting of the Information Sciences and Technologies Study Group (ISAT) which was reviewing technology issues. ISAT concluded that while certain technological safeguards (such as hiding individual identification when sorting though millions of records, or blocking access to unauthorized persons) could be used, many members were skeptical that they would really work. Ironically, they also proposed "Strong Audit mechanisms" – in other words, built-in means of watching the watchers.

Of course, one can also point out the technical shortcomings of the kinds of technique used in TIA. Like some surveillance methods discussed earlier, commercial databases tend to have high error rates, but, in addition to this, so little is known about terrorists that they are hard to distinguish from the rest of the population. Because the idea of data-mining is to know in advance who may be a terrorist, such distinctions are crucial. Other techniques such as biometric identification are intrinsic aspects of the TIA program, which, as we have seen, is also problematic. DARPA initiated the "ID at a distance" system to positively identity people by gait or face recognition and would like to see this linked with a national ID system to simplify the process of tracking individuals over multiple information sources. Each of these has already been discussed in terms of its merits and shortcomings.

What the appearance of TIA and related programs indicate is that the US administration, through the Homeland Security Department and through the Pentagon's TIA initiative, is determined to find new ways of tracking down terrorists, whatever it takes. Previously separate databases and jurisdictions are being elided if not merged. Currently, already existing consumer and related data are being mined to try to predict terrorist activity. It appears that they are doing so using methods whose record is far from successful and that override previous limitations on personal data-gathering operations. The American military is expanding its activities into domestic security in unprecedented ways. The barrier between domestic and overseas intelligence gathering, erected when the CIA was created in 1947, is being steadily dismantled. Lessons supposedly learned in the McCarthy era are apparently forgotten or conveniently ignored.[7] Surveillance methods and processes are being integrated.

Convergence, Codes, and Categories

Although it can be exaggerated, the use of computers and telecommunications undoubtedly helps hasten both the growth and the integration of surveillance. Indeed, the use of similar kinds of technical systems and software, plus the decisive shift toward a consumer phase of capitalism, meant that in the later part of the twentieth century a subtle transformation occurred. The surveillance state expanded to become the surveillance society. Or rather, several factors made it possible, feasible, and eventually desirable for organizations to engage in surveillance practices that had nothing directly to do with the state but which, as the aftermath of 9/11 shows, the state would be able to use to its purposes. The garnering of personal data in a systematic fashion, by organizations that wish to influence, manage, or control those under surveillance, is no longer merely the domain of agencies such as the police, security forces, or taxation officials.

In both public and private, state and civil society settings, surveillance practices are increasingly integrated. George Orwell once warned against a centralized totalitarian surveillance state, in which Big Brother held sway through a regime of fear and uncertainty. This now becomes possible through system integration, not necessarily centralization. Such totalitarian tendencies are always present within advanced bureaucratic surveillance systems. But in the twentieth century the memory of fascism and Nazism was sufficiently strong to ensure that democratic societies were alert to those dangers. The combination of fading memories, with alternative, and more subtle, means of surveillance, which are also suffused with the spirit of high-tech hubris and thus carry an intrinsic attraction for those who wish to side with "progress," made the risks less palpable at the end of the twentieth century.

In the 1990s faith in high technology received a huge boost in the shape of the internet and the World Wide Web, as well as private intranets that are in some ways more powerful than the "public" internet. Aside from the hype about "cyberspace," which frequently forgets the very social and material bases and consequences of "online activity,"[8] the socially significant development for surveillance processes was twofold. "Networking" became an everyday reality, connecting all manner of systems and creating millions of potential linkages. And "searchable databases"[9] were designed that could be operated by any ordinary user without knowledge of computer science or software architectures. Collecting data for, and obtaining access to, massive stores of information, including personal data, became an everyday occurrence.

This does not mean that all the data that could be collected is collected, or that literally anyone may obtain access to the computer systems that hold the data. Many technical, cultural, economic, and legal barriers to such activities existed at the end of the twentieth century. Although many companies and government departments were keen to realize the potential of the amazing new technologies, they did not or could not do so. Those circumstances were to change dramatically and decisively on September 11, 2001.

In his book, *Code and Other Laws of Cyberspace*, Lawrence Lessig makes the point – contested among those who believe the internet to be a "realm of freedom" – that cyberspace is governed by its codes. In other words, the interests of creators and users are already built into the network, through its software protocols and configurations. Power is present in the very constitution of the internet – and in the many analogues of the Internet that make up the electronically mediated world of social relations called cyberspace. Among other things, this means that software used for sorting behaviors, preferences, and practices operates in particular ways.

This fact makes the surveillance done by computer systems far more efficient and powerful than any direct observation by neighbors or workplace supervisors, in principle, at least. In practice, the effectiveness and efficiency of such systems varies dramatically. The potential efficiency of computerized surveillance does not mean, I hasten to add, that direct observation is not also effective for certain purposes. Rather, this argument simply states that much surveillance today is different from what occurred before monitoring became computer-assisted. Early forms of surveillance picked up only specific data, watched only particular activities. Today's assumes, increasingly, that all monitoring will produce searchable records.[10]

The surveillance situation altered once it became possible to extend the "gaze" from national state and capitalist corporation record-keeping and monitoring to include all kinds of everyday transactions. The records of Mohammed Atta, on CCTV tapes and digital logs, were collected not because he was doing anything unusual or deviant. Just the opposite. Data-gathering is routine, generalized, and distributed across almost every sphere of daily life. Once those records are examined, however, it may become incumbent on "data-subjects" to account for their activities. All data-subjects lose their innocence and we all enter a more "fish-bowl"-like world where our business is open to the scrutiny of others. But this is not all: the advent of searchable databases means that records may be assembled from different sources to create portraits or at least "profiles" of individuals and groups. This is why the codes by which the categories are constructed are so important.

In the commercial sphere, constructing profiles of consumers is seen as a way of making marketing more efficient. You can "get to know" your customers better, and even form "relationships" with them through knowing their preferences for this brand of boots, that color of clothing, or the other type of movie. But even here, there are other effects. The range of choices for consumers may in fact be narrowed, and the precisely targeted advertising – for instance from pop-up online ads relating to web sites recently visited – may manipulate desires, albeit subtly.

As well, profiling offers further opportunities for discriminating between different kinds of consumer, privileging some with special service or discounts, and ignoring others with less purchasing power. As Oscar Gandy observes, this discriminatory process flies in the face of the ideal of equality, because it extends opportunity based simply on ability to pay.[11] It turns surveillance into a form of "social sorting" that classifies people according to criteria originating in the agency that surveills. Who does that coding is again a crucial question – and not only in the consumer sphere, as we shall see in a moment.

Technically, the coding occurs thus. Digital information is reduced to binary codes of ones and zeros that make it easy to record, store, and retrieve data. In order to create databases, however, data must be assigned to "fields." These are inflexible variables that form the building blocks of databases. Otherwise diverse and complex realities are broken down into artificial, discrete categories. This means that records are stripped-down for particular purposes – matters such as context, motive, and desire are often screened out in the quest for automation. What is often vital background information, or the views and commitments that might be admitted in a conversation, are discarded from the coded data image. (As I say, the idea of "relationships" is hollow here.) To gather data, computers need sets of instructions – algorithms – that are translated into software. Software comprises connected and coded algorithms.

Algorithmic surveillance depends on such coding. For instance, when CCTV cameras are hooked up to computer systems to enable "facial recognition" to occur, the coding sorts faces in front of the cameras by comparing them with those in a database.[12] No longer does an operator have to decide whether or not the face appearing on the screen is that of a "known offender." The algorithm decides between one image and the next. Needless to say, the loss of human discretion is not necessarily an unmitigated improvement,[13] but this is what distinguishes one system from the other.

If one considers border controls, it is clear that the processes of decision-making about who should be allowed in and who should not have depended on forms of categorization for many decades. This is the backdrop to, as well as part of the explanation for, the ways in which automated and semi-automated systems are coded today. In a study of airport controls in the 1980s, for example,

Janet Gilboy shows how categories are not merely formed by rational and cognitive distinctions, but by the immediate situations in the agencies and offices where decisions are taken.[14] High and low risk, positive and negative categories have been the daily grids of inspectors for many years. Certain groups are dubious (such as "nannies") and others (such as business travelers) low risk. Some countries of origin are thought of as producing benign and others as producing troublesome travelers. Crucially, the designation of high risk may alter – as it did in the course of Gilboy's study – according to circumstance.

After 9/11 new categories appeared rapidly – or, rather, old ones were revived. Heightened attention was given to Arab and Muslim travelers. Much attention has been paid to the issue of "racial profiling" but it is clear that considerable controversy surrounds the topic. For some, the new "racial profiling" is an extension of the common notion, known all too well by some groups who live in urban areas, that "driving while black" is likely to attract police attention. A high-profile controversy on just this issue ignited in Toronto in October 2002. Since 9/11, the new category for suspicion is "flying while Arab."[15] Immediately after the attacks, several pilots on scheduled flights in and from the USA simply refused to carry passengers from Middle Eastern backgrounds, usually to the embarrassment of their airlines.[16] Even at our little local airport in Kingston, Ontario, I was recently made aware of different treatment accorded to a family evidently originating from the Indian sub-continent, when I – the white male – went straight through security checks without delay and they had their bag-handles swabbed for traces of explosives.

Many examples of "racial profiling" are as crude as these stories suggest, but in other cases technological assistance is sought. In October 2002 the American FBI was still engaged with 24-hour monitoring of young Muslim men, checking their phone calls, their email and internet use, their credit card charges and travel routes.[17] Unsurprisingly, groups such as the American-Arab Anti-Discrimination Committee have received many complaints that young men of Arab descent or Muslim faith are being treated as suspicious, if not dangerous. But even these examples do not necessarily point to algorithmic surveillance that operates using "racial" or "religious" categories. Seen with other measures, however, it is hard to believe that such "racial profiling" will not also be coded-in to software. The passenger pre-screening system, CAPPS II, is likely to be augmented by "trusted traveler" schemes using biometrics, for which Ben Gurion Airport in Tel Aviv is offered as a model. That system is based on clear but contentious "ethnic" distinctions.[18]

Another way that "racial profiling" may occur within automated systems is through airport scanners that check names against "watch lists." Security agencies that already include "Arab" or "Muslim" within their surveillance categories are likely simply to extend these into the scanners. As we saw, marketing devices such as "Customer Relationship Marketing" are now being retooled for profiling suspected terrorists and, given the origins of the September 11 attackers, such profiles are unlikely to exclude "racial" and "religious" criteria. Thus, whether the profile is a crude "flying while Arab" in the judgment of an over-anxious pilot, or the product of a more sophisticated software tool, the effects are similar. The code becomes a means of discrimination which, when linked with stereotypes, produces gratuitously unequal treatment for certain groups of people.

A New Governance

New surveillance techniques may involve high technology, but those technologies do not themselves explain what is happening. Even the convergence of different kinds of surveillance, which brings together data from marketing endeavors and from policing and intelligence, is merely enabled and facilitated by developments in communication and information technologies, not caused by them. Especially after 9/11, it is important to see how responses to the attacks fit with already emerging trends. Some of those trends relate to shifts within military strategy, and the rise of "virtual war," which among other things make its victims less visible. But other trends relate to what David Garland calls the "new culture of crime control"[19] and they help us see what is going on in much richer sociological terms.

By "new," Garland means the past 30 years or so. To explore this, he describes fundamental shifts in social life and expectations in "late modern" societies, along with the swing to free market, socially conservative governments since the 1980s. Increasing mobility, changing families and households, suburbanization, new media, and democratization of social and cultural life are all woven into the tale he tells. His analysis focuses mainly on the USA and the UK, but it has many strong echoes elsewhere. It leads him to conclude that an older "social welfare" view of crime and social control is being challenged by two different criminologies. If the old model was "modern," the newer ones are "late modern" criminologies of everyday life, and "anti-modern" criminologies of the other.

Garland argues that while the older "penal welfarism" sees criminality as rooted in social deprivation, and offenders as needing to be reformed and reintegrated in society, the everyday life approach looks, rather, at social situations and settings to see how opportunities for crime can be reduced. This happens by developing a network of unobtrusive situational controls that create order without disturbing the flow of events. This is exactly what was happening in surveillance before 9/11 and such "unobtrusive controls" are now being intensified as a result of the attacks.

As Garland says, these latter criminologies are largely amoral and technological; their "conception of social order is a matter not of shared values but of smart arrangements that minimize the opportunities for disruption and deviance."[20] If the system works more smoothly, then the fact that it might exclude whole groups of people is not a major concern. Discriminatory use of police powers and civil liberties violations of the poor and of minorities is not unexpected. Social and economic conditions conducive to crime are not so much rejected as repaired. A kind of mechanical failure, not social injustice, is the problem.

The other challenge to penal welfarism comes from those who wish to question the values of late modern societies. If everyday life criminology de-dramatizes crime, making it routine and unremarkable, this challenge re-dramatizes it with melodramatic rhetoric and by placing around it a frame of war and social defense.[21] In this case, the problem is moral, not mechanical. Evil takes shape in particular persons who are other than us, and who have no calls on our care. They deserve what they get by way of punishment and should not expect to be "understood." Those who do not fit should be excluded. But just like the criminology of everyday life, this one focuses on control, on the ordinariness of crime, and on a rejection of penal-welfarism.

Again, the resonance with the aftermath of 9/11 is strong. We have already seen how the spectacle of the burning, collapsing towers fed into the synoptic reinforcement of surveillance. The now (in)famous presidential speeches about an "axis of evil" and about "those who are not for us are against us" also echo the "criminology of the other" viewpoint. Swashbuckling words and overt denunciation of whole populations go hand-in-hand with a willingness to place suspects in a Cuban prison camp, detain many hundreds of others, and subject yet more to systematic surveillance, despite the protests against ethnic unfairness and religious slurs.

Garland makes one other vital observation that affects the analysis of surveillance, that these shifts also reflect a drift from a social to an economic mode of reasoning. Penal welfarism was based on the idea that crime has social origins and social solutions (which idea does not, of course, obviate any focus on moral responsibility). Today, the allocation of resources and distribution of powers seems much more significant. Costs and effectiveness now loom front and center in these debates. Managerialism, with its accounting methods and evaluations, creates cost-benefit scales throughout the system. It fits with the view that crime is an externality or the outcome of rational choices. And it is expressed in initiatives that take their cues from insurance companies or private security firms. Safety and security are commodities that must be paid for.

If one follows only the technological trajectory of surveillance, the nuances of the story, and indeed some of its deeper themes, will be missed. The city once had walls and gates to keep unwanted persons out or, in more modern times, straight streets so that troublemakers could easily be seen by police. Theorists such as Paul Virilio have noted the ways in which a new "vision machine" has become central to control in contemporary societies, and he makes some insightful comments about the effects of this as more and more aspects of daily life are made visible to others.[22] Mechanizing visibility through the use of cameras and the like may make the population more amenable to control, but it also takes away trust. Gilles Deleuze, too, makes brief but trenchant comment on the rise of "societies of control" whose cities are now subject to sets of "audio-visual protocols" for all who would pass through.[23] Others have proposed that forms of "digital rule" follow from this, that have implications for contemporary social control.[24]

It is at this point that the "assemblage" becomes relevant. In the surveillant assemblage the body is broken down into bits of data that can be collected, stored, analyzed, and recombined. In the first place, the body is neither punished nor held in check. The bits of data may literally be from the body, such as fingerprints, iris scans, blood samples, or facial images. Or they may be drawn from behaviors and transactions in which the body is involved, albeit in a secondary or indirect fashion. Hence bank withdrawals, phone calls, card swipes, and PIN presentation may also yield other bits of data relating to the body in question. The use of commercial databases by the police, and of data collected by the census or taxation departments by marketing companies, may be thought of as rhizomic. They are enabled by network technologies and encouraged by the commodification of information.

The illuminating metaphor of the rhizome and the helpful concept of assemblage permit some theoretical purchase on the growth of today's surveillance systems. The modern world may be a society of strangers, but no one was able to maintain their anonymity for long. Bodies may well have "disappeared" as it became possible to do things at a distance, without direct involvement or intervention, but they were made to reappear courtesy of surveillance.[25] Or rather, bits of data originating in bodies appeared, first as bureaucratic, then as electronic proxies for those bodies, standing in for enfleshed persons. Surveillance occurred in departments of the state and in agencies such as policing, in workplaces, and in the marketplace. But as the value of data to other organizations became apparent, and as technologies were sought and designed that allowed such data to circulate, so those discrete surveillance agencies were able to cooperate, and their activities to be coordinated. Surveillance practices and processes were already converging before 9/11; the process accelerated afterwards.

Terrorism and Surveillance

Social scientists and historians are sometimes guilty of exaggerating changes that occur in social organization. The rhetorical point made by a title that starts "From . . ." and is completed with ". . . to" is seductively simple but frequently faulty. Those who have noted the subtle shifts towards rhizomic assemblages that draw all into the surveillance web can sometimes give the impression that, in the tilt toward the assemblage, the apparatus has been left far behind. It is true that the assemblage is no respecter of persons, in that you do not have to commit a crime or buck a trend to have your details recorded. But it is decidedly mistaken to think that the raw powers of the sovereign state cannot on occasion be invoked. The state apparatus is still there, even when the surveillant assemblage is present. Indeed, the two are undergoing integration.

Certainly, one of the biggest structural alterations with which twenty-first century societies of the global north have to grapple is the diminished power of the state. This is expressed in specific ways, above all in the power to provide security for citizens or a level of social control that makes social life not only tolerable but also enjoyable.[26] Centralized command and coercion can no longer work, any more than centralized health and welfare bureaucracies can. As Michel Foucault argues, other means of governance emerged during the twentieth century – indeed, he invented a new word for them: "governmentality."[27] Others besides the state itself are enlisted into the processes of creating order, of providing incentives for certain kinds of behaviors, and of fostering new modes of cooperation between different agencies. As the organizations and associations of civil society are pulled in to fulfill the tasks of governmentality, so their methods of data-processing and networking also become part of the larger surveillance picture.

Little surprise, then, that the US administration and its allies are working towards new forms of data-sharing in the war against terrorism. One report asks for a domestic intelligence center within the new Department of Homeland Security which would, they say, both protect privacy and prevent terror.[28] This would obtain data from both federal and state sources, plus private sector databases. Tips from local and state agencies, along with businesses, are regarded by the report as "the real frontlines of homeland security." Also, the counter-terrorism sections of the FBI and the CIA are being moved into a single complex to coordinate the analysis and tracking of information. The Terrorist Threat Information Center is intended to create a more integrated system, though critics fear that the CIA will have a new domestic spying role.[29] Similar initiatives have been proposed elsewhere, too. Indeed, as we shall see in the next chapter, such proposals include the sharing of relevant data across national borders.

It is important to understand what such data-sharing entails. Although the technologies are not the prime mover of social change, they do bring with them some specific capacities and styles of operation. Above all, coding makes possible certain kinds of classification, which categorize people and populations according to the purposes of the organization. Call centers, for example, prioritize calls, depending on what they are worth to the company, and internet services are often similarly classed.[30] These are significant means of social sorting, of digital discrimination. They are thus vulnerable to stereotyping, redlining (and now, "weblining"), and other kinds of unequal treatment. Without very careful safeguards in place, these will continue to exacerbate already existing inequalities of income, gender, "race," or religion. In the convergence of different and previously discrete surveillance systems, it is this feature – social sorting by searchable database – that the new surveillance assemblage has at its core.

The attacks of 9/11 did not produce the new surveillance. It was already spreading steadily, sending out its shoots through national and international infrastructures of electronic communication and through alliances of agencies and organizations once quite separate from the state. But the systems were boosted by 9/11, as the criminologies of both everyday life and of the other found new justifications for mundane controls and for exclusionary tactics. They both feed on the belief in technical fixes and their concomitant downplaying of labor-intensive solutions. And they distract even more from attempts to understand and address the causes of terrorism.

The convergence and integration of surveillance before 9/11 seems set to continue, to deepen, and to widen as a result of the attacks. Social sorting and digital discrimination will characterize surveillance more and more, as a result of state-sponsored initiatives to integrate systems in the war against terrorism. This springs from a well-meaning effort to second-guess who might be plotting violence and to counteract the networking of asymmetric power. But it is far from obvious that the desired results will appear. Nonetheless, there will be results. Unless some other dramatic intervention occurs, the surveillance trends discussed here will further bolster the general culture of control.

5

Globalizing Surveillance

"Terrorism is the dark side of globalization."
Colin Powell[1]

September 11, 2001 was a world event but it was also a globalized event. It had impacts throughout the world because it was a product of globalization. Those impacts stimulated further globalizing processes. Among these were increased surveillance flows that presage new patterns of power and social arrangements. Air traffic, foreign nationals, and networked messages were involved in the attacks, so airline passenger data, immigration records, and telephone and email logs became the focus of surveillance attention. International police efforts to hunt down terrorist cells of al-Qaeda members involve integrated communication and data-sharing schemes. Just as the attacks had been planned and coordinated at a distance, so the responses also link remote databases and information sources in real-time.

One consequence of 9/11 is the tightening of airport security. Flights originating in Canada, for example, are obliged to send passenger data on ahead of the plane, to the destination airport in the USA. The coordination of international police activities is also being upgraded so that responses to potential suspects and emergencies are quicker. Such developments mean that more and more personal data flows around the world, crossing borders at a rapid rate. It also means that borders themselves become "delocalized"[2] as efforts are made to make check travelers before they reach physical borders or ports of entry. Images and information circulate through different departments, looping back and forth in commercial, policing, and government networks. Surveillance records, once kept in fixed filing cabinets and dealing in data focused on persons in specific places, are now fluid, flowing, and global. These consequences are properly "globalized" in the sense that they signal new patterns of social activity and novel social arrangements, which are less constrained by geography.[3] The "delocalized border" is a prime example of globalized surveillance.

September 11 and its aftermath has everything to do with globalization, which both enabled the event to happen and provides the conduits for its consequences. Globalization extends to encompass the world by the process in which things are increasingly done at a distance. So western industry, commerce, entertainment, law, and education touch lives in far-flung parts of the globe. They bring *Dallas*, Coke, Big Macs, Nike, and GAP clothing into the streets and homes of people who can scarcely afford them and who have no concept of the culture that produces them. Only in a globalized world could people so geographically remote from each other have such a strong sense that the process is something negative that is being done to them. Yet this is just how many Islamic and Arabic-speaking groups (not to mention others) think about the West. Courtesy of new communications technologies, business transactions, TV shows, and travel schedules can be coordinated in real time. The 9/11 plotters depended on this both for carrying out the attacks and for ensuring their media coverage.

Globalization is puzzling and paradoxical. It puts a premium on movement and mobility in a world where only the rich – and refugees – can travel.[4] The one wants to, the other has to. It is often taken to be about westernization of the world, or the Americanization of commerce and culture. It is true that the USA is in a sense the dominant globalizing force. Equally true that much globalization obliges people to come to terms with western culture. But in fact there are many globalizations, some of which successfully bypass the USA altogether. And the globalization of surveillance is no exception to the paradoxical rule. The free flows of technology, persons, data, images, pests, information, waste, ideas, and, now, terrorist networks that both constitute and characterize globalization are very hard to slow down or to stop. The world of the internet, with its built-in capacity to seek ways around obstacles and to continue working even when some nodes are taken out, typifies these global flows. Having set globalization processes in motion, they now have a momentum of their own. Any attempt to make borders less porous, to check and to contain personal and population data, does so against the current of these incessant flows.

Colin Powell is right to state that "terrorism is the dark side of globalization" but it is important to take the phrase at full value. The moon has a "dark side" too, intrinsically related to it, and without which it would no longer exist. Benjamin Barber's argument about jihad and McWorld picks up the sense of mutual dependence of "holy war" and consumer globalization.[5] McWorld fosters sterility and anomie – "normlessness" – that produces quests for certainty such as fundamentalism, neo-fascism, and anti-immigration sentiment in different countries. This is not something affecting merely the "Muslim world," but which has a variety of effects in different parts of the planet.[6] McWorld and jihad mutually reinforce each other in the "new world disorder," and this curious dialectical attraction sucks states and strategies into strange alliances. Among these, some reluctant Muslims have been driven to support the attacks and some unlikely countries have capitulated to "control creep" with new surveillance measures.[7]

In this chapter, the augmenting of already existing global surveillance such as the Echelon system is noted, as well as new systems that are being established after the attacks. Given the importance of airline and airport security since 9/11, particular attention is paid to attempts to increase surveillance of travelers on the move through the world's air corridors. Other paradoxes of global surveillance are also presented, especially those raised by the free flows of data. And some conclusions are suggested about the nature of worldwide surveillance after September 11. Those who fear the advent of some centralized global surveillance system – a world brain tracking and monitoring our every move – are missing the point. The globalization of surveillance is as unevenly spread as many other kinds of globalization. Globalizing surveillance affects the global north in particular, but has ramifications for the global south as well. However, paranoia about world control should not be exchanged for complacency. As on the national level, so at the global – surveillance is increasingly integrated between previously discrete systems.

Globalization, Terrorism, and Surveillance

Globalization of a sort existed in the nineteenth century and before. But it was really the improvements in transport and communications of the twentieth century that gave us globalization as we now know it. Indeed, the term only gained widespread use, for and against, in the 1990s. Only from that decade onwards did politicians vie with each other's competing claims that the only economically desirable enterprises were global ones. And only in the 1990s did serious resistance (often mistakenly called "anti-globalization"[8]) movements take off. As with all such concepts, globalization is slippery, both in terms of what it includes (can it exclude anything?) and in terms of its political charge. Some background is necessary if the term is to be used intelligently and fruitfully, but my focus here is guided by the need to consider specifically the globalization of surveillance. Three views form a useful starting point.

Wide-eyed accounts of the new global order may be wearing thin, but there are plenty who still take the view that globalization is the progressive wave of the future.[9] In this first scenario, capitalism triumphs yet again, this time through the creation of a single global economy in which capital – and other – flows wash over national governments which are left helplessly in their wake. The nation-state is shown to have been a temporary experiment; its erstwhile sovereign power is now replaced by local economic management. Politics is a thing of the past.

Against such hype, secondly, some social scientists have responded in kind, issuing blinkered bulletins about business as usual. They reassure us that the nation-state is alive and will thrive, right into the twenty-first century. Far from being on its last gasp, linked up to a life-support machine, the state still initiates and regulates economies. Moreover, the naysayers maintain, there is no unified global world emerging; rather, nation-states are splitting into fragments and factions, each presiding over cultural and religious differences that may erupt in conflict at any time. Such differences also relate to massive disparities of wealth and access to the means of growth.

Yet other theorists argue – thirdly, and more soberly – that we are witnessing a global restructuring of political economies in which nation-states are gradually adopting new roles, and corporations are indeed "going global." But it is crucial to note that different processes occur on different scales of activity: regional, national, municipal, and local. This makes the emerging picture very complex, not to mention volatile. In this view, globalization revitalizes the local, because groups at different levels have to respond to and contribute to change beyond old borders. And it also does so using new media. As Manuel Castells observes, the truly globalized corporation is the one operating simultaneously in many different parts of the world, and whose activities are coordinated in real time.[10]

These factors are important for understanding surveillance today, and especially since 9/11. Activities coordinated in real time rely on advanced computer-communications networks. Information and data are among the "flows" that are the life-blood of globalization. As more and more activities spill over the borders of nation-states and conventional economic areas, so some familiar features of social life, such as crime, reappear on a globalized scale. And while some nations wish to increase flows of people such as migrant labor, tourists, or refugees, others wish to slow or stop the flows. To keep track of activities, both legal and illegal, the same electronic media are used to monitor, record, identify, and check persons and groups that are involved in the flows.

Government departments, corporations, non-government organizations (NGOs), and other entities are involved not only in the globalized flows, but also in observing and managing them. Moreover, when increased personal and group data start to circulate, so do questions about appropriate ways of handling the fuller flows of personal data. Do the "fair information practices" of one country apply in another? Will this country trade with one that has different standards and expectations for dealing with data? These sorts of question, and then the policies that go with them, also "go global." Hence, the globalization of surveillance and, usually not far behind, of data-protection policies.

However, these flows are not uncontested. They exist in a world that is undergoing a multifaceted restructuring process, and where the stakes – economic, political, cultural, military – are high. The search for higher speeds of transfer, for instantaneous transactions, for a "global time" that annihilates the time zones invented in the 1880s means little to billions of the world's inhabitants who happen to live in the global south. Not surprisingly, many of those are sufficiently aware of the gap that separates them from the global north to feel that they are victims, not victors, in a globalizing world. As Zygmunt Bauman suggests, globalization brings with it some perfectly understandable discontents for those with eyes to see them.[11] Writing prior to 9/11, he was especially concerned about the (paradoxical!) progressive breakdown of communication between global elites and the localized rest.

Some of those discontents became blindingly clear – if they were not already so – on September 11, 2001. The Pentagon is the symbol of global military power, matched by the symbol of global economic and media power, the *World* Trade Center. Jihad, as Benjamin Barber might have put it, had struck an anticipated blow against *McWorld*.[12] Those conduits of communication carrying the free market message were savagely sabotaged, with a subsequent scattering not unlike that following the fabled fall of another tower – the Tower of Babel.[13] The new global business community, speaking the language of "profit maximization, shareholder value, efficiency, competition, and progress . . . without limits or boundaries"[14] truly had its language confused on 9/11. The globalization of surveillance cannot responsibly be discussed without recalling this context.

Globalized Surveillance

There is no doubt that the Cold War prompted the twentieth century's massive expansion of international surveillance systems. Indeed, it is true to say that the Cold War was *conducted* primarily through various kinds of espionage, undercover agencies, and the range of cloak-and-dagger activities that became the staple of several famous spy movies. Cold warriors were intelligence experts. British agents in Russia were celebrated even when they were known to be double-crossing their various paymasters, and in the USA, the Cold War was perhaps best known in its notorious McCarthyite era when no stone was left unturned in the insidious search for the "enemy within." One might be forgiven for saying that history seems to be repeating itself since 9/11 – just replace the surveillance target "communist" with "terrorist."

Of course, history does not repeat itself, and one also must note some divergences from the old Cold War surveillance practices. Globalization is helping to transform the way that "security" is understood, from "guns and bombs" to a whole raft of areas from the environment to finance.[15] Also, where "ideology" was once seen as the problem, now "ethnicity" is the issue. Once, the USA was the main proponent of Cold War doctrines. Now a number of European countries, plus Japan and Australia – in fact most countries in the global north – are part of the new security state whose policies tend to view all Arabs and Muslims as potential terrorists.

During the Cold War period, already existing networks of international communications interception were consolidated above all in the creation of the so-called "UKUSA" agreement which, as the acronym suggests, involved Britain and America as central players, but with the latter as senior partner. In the name of international security, a clandestine community of intelligence workers, with huge funding and extensive infrastructure, established linked satellite stations around the world to keep track of global communications. This community reports back to a virtually unaccountable organization, the US National Security Agency, based in Maryland.

Within this, the system known as Echelon became best known in recent years – but not because its activities were publicized, or even acknowledged by its founders and operators. Indeed, public knowledge of the existence of systems like this owes much to the dogged persistence of investigative journalists such as Duncan Campbell (UK) and Nicky Hager (New Zealand).[16] In his book, *Secret Power*, the latter documented a time when former prime minister David Lange proudly announced that New Zealand's national security would never be in the hands of a foreign government. The occasion for the announcement was the opening of a new facility where such foreign (US) control was actually the case. Even he, the minister responsible for security and intelligence, did not know that New Zealand was part of an international electronic spy network.

The old world of illegal bug-planting has been superseded by one in which the new interception networks operate by means of vacuuming in vast quantities of data from which sought messages are siphoned off using "intelligent filters." Key words trigger hits among the various telephone, fax, and email communications that are then tagged and sent on to the requesting country within the network. Unlike the original Cold War systems, however, Echelon is used as much for non-military as military purposes. Governments, organizations of all sorts, and businesses may be targeted by its sorting devices.[17] Thus the Cold War intelligence systems, though enormous in scope, are now far more extensive and technologically sophisticated, and include all manner of groups within their remit.

Based in Europe, a similar system has grown out of the collaborative process that began in the small town of Schengen in Luxembourg in 1985. At the time, the idea was to mutually recognize visas, and to strengthen police cooperation between member countries. By 1999 this Agreement had grown into a proposed system for registration and surveillance of large population groups, and the agreement was folded into the European Union (EU), with the addition of at least two non-EU members, Norway and Iceland.[18] The tentacles of this system stretch from the Arctic Circle to the Mediterranean. This makes an amalgamated police-based data network which enables individuals to be singled out for specific scrutiny, and large populations sorted for further surveillance and "special treatment."[19] Whereas Echelon intercepts communications, and so is future-oriented, the Schengen Information System (SIS) stores personal data on criminals and "suspects" and thus is past-oriented. Echelon has clandestine origins; SIS was agreed upon democratically in the European Union. SIS may be used for "public order" and/or "state security" – as seen from its political uses in detaining Greenpeace activists and other demonstrators. Many aspects of its operation are also hidden, secretive. Notice that all these systems were operational (at least in part) *prior* to 9/11.

As with other forms of surveillance, 9/11 did not prompt the introduction of communications interception.

This is surely one of the oldest methods of surveillance, which has a long history of use for law enforcement and military intelligence in particular. During the twentieth century, these were increasingly rationalized, and eventually enhanced by computerization. Indeed, many of the surveillance technologies which are now visible in policing and even in marketing found their origin in military intelligence systems. Policing has in this way, as in others, become increasingly militarized,[20] and it must be said that the language of "strategy" and "targeting" is not absent from marketing either.[21]

Indeed, not long after 9/11 it became clear that forms of business analysis were being retooled for anti-terrorist purposes.[22] As we saw in chapter 4, Customer Relationship Management (CRM), data-mining, and data-warehousing, which began life as marketing devices, have been used successfully by government departments. At first this was to target groups in areas such as taxes, utilities, and health care, but now they are sought by policing and intelligence agencies. CRM helps firms to analyze customer data for marketing decision-making, and is supported by data-mining, to discover sequences, associations, classification, clustering, and forecasting. Data-warehousing also enhances the usefulness of such personal data by cleansing it to correct differences and inaccuracies between data sources and data models. The aim is to understand customer preferences, create profiles, and predict customer behavior – a task closely analogous to what is said to be required for anti-terrorist activity.

Computerization makes possible the narrowing of searches for delinquent communications. Combined with satellite tracking stations, and now internet surveillance, this creates a situation in which massive power is vested in "intelligence" service of all kinds. The searchable database is key to this, and the well-known search engine, Google, demonstrates the ease with which, given a few clues, numerous likely "hits" can be made very quickly. It also shows how effective – at least in principle – the internet and World Wide Web are in facilitating remote searches.

After 9/11 many mass media outlets drew attention to the existence of Carnivore, the internet surveillance system already used by the FBI, and to Echelon, the far larger system for international monitoring of all communication. It came as a surprise to many that such sophisticated search engines already existed, powered by huge "dictionaries" that check messages for key words and contexts in quest of suspicious or risky communications. These are used not only for military or terrorist threats, either. Increasingly, they may be used by police departments trying to prepare for protests such as those by "anti-globalization" groups, and also as a means of technological and commercial intelligence, to raise the stakes of economic competition.

One might justifiably ask how the attacks of 9/11 were not detected, given the huge intelligence infrastructure that was in place. FBI assistant director Ron Dick noted that the hijackers had used the internet to good effect.[23] Internet Service Providers (ISPs) handed over records of hundreds of messages sent from PCs and public sites such as libraries, in the USA and internationally. They were unencrypted messages and used simple open codes. The National Security Agency response to growing internet traffic has been to multiply the power of its storage and search facilities, from a petabyte (roughly eight times the information in the Library of Congress) to a petaplex (20 million gigabytes) system. But it is not clear that this will work any better than what was in place before 9/11, because the problem of correlating diverse information rises exponentially as ever more communications are intercepted.

The point has been made a number of times since 9/11 that it was not lack of information so much as the lack of analysis of information which created the surprise element of the attacks. But while better analysis, and improved integration between information holders, could potentially produce other outcomes, a more fundamental problem hampers efforts to predict terrorist activity: terrorism is itself networked. As Ron Deibert and Janice Stein observe, movements like al-Qaeda are not based in states, are not territorial at all, and are distributed.[24] To pit centralized (or at least integrated) state powers of surveillance against a network is not merely inappropriate, it may be counter-productive. The most vital terrorist communications may be missed (al-Qaeda groups use, but are not dependent on, the internet), and the increased volume of data may simply slow the response by producing a glut. Targeted security, which Deibert and Stein suggest as an alterna-tive, would deny opportunities for terrorist network activ-ity without infringing on civil rights as present methods do.

Several other interesting issues are raised by increased communications interception, and particularly internet sur-veillance, following 9/11. It demonstrates, first, the ways in which national governments and corporations are working together more closely, such that companies may do "police" work, both on their own account and for the authorities. Law enforcers have increased by five times their demands for information from email providers and ISPs in the USA.[25] Concerns about "privacy" in this area, which were growing before 9/11, seem to coexist, at least in the rhetoric, with a new willingness of companies to cooperate in the "war against terror." Companies start to comply with requests for data even before the warrant has been issued, which suggests that an ongoing state of "emergency" has been accepted. Under the US PATRIOT

Act customer payment records can be subpoenaed to find the ID behind an email address, clickstreams can be monitored, and messages can be read or listened to in real time. Similar provisions are in force elsewhere.[26]

Secondly, the US government in particular has taken on a stronger policing role in other countries. Foreign hackers can be prosecuted by the USA under the PATRIOT Act when computers in the USA or abroad are attacked. Because such a large volume of global internet traffic flows through the USA (80 percent of Asian, African, and South American access points, for example),[27] it can be criminalized under US law.

Thirdly, the upshot of post-9/11 surveillance is that more and more mundane transactions and conversations of everyday life are under scrutiny as never before. The new provisions may not catch terrorists but they could complicate life for others, especially as they are monitored, classified, and evaluated. In the UK, for example, where the Regulation of Investigatory Powers Act already had sweeping capacities to obtain communications data without a court order, anti-terrorist legislation allows these to be retained for longer.[28] When one considers that the meaning of a web site or of search words is different from, say, a phone number (which gives little away in itself), it is clear that captured communicational data is also more and more detailed. Web sites and email addresses are already linked with other data, accessible from any terminal. To connect phone numbers with more than names and street addresses requires specific searches.

Needless to say, these conclusions about the growing range of surveillance technologies are not uncontroversial. The ever-optimistic *Wired Magazine* still believes that "Little Brothers" will answer back, that ordinary people will empower themselves with their own technologies, that the US Constitution still stands as a bulwark of liberty, and that the sheer volume of new gadgets will countervail against government power.[29] But the larger context – discussed earlier and in the conclusion of this book – must also be borne in mind before such sanguine conclusions can be confirmed.

Airline Passenger Data

Airports are crucial channels of mobility for the global citizens of the twenty-first century. They are points of entry and exit for tourists, businesspersons, workers, students, and, of course, for some refugees as well. The scale of operations is huge. International passenger travel increased twelvefold in the second half of the twentieth century[30] and the vast majority of this is accounted for in air travel. In the USA alone there are two million daily air travelers on 20,000 flights.[31] Airports are "placeless" sites of temporary sojourn, air-lock chambers for nomadic executives or sun-seekers. But they have profound social and political significance, particularly in personal data-handling.

Because airports have to process so many passengers, commercial industries have grown up around air travel. Not only travel agencies themselves, but many other enterprises have also sprung up. These include networks of car rental companies, hotel chains, restaurants, and the now ubiquitous airport shopping precinct – the mall for the mobile. Airports are concerned with consumption, which goes far beyond just airline ticketing and air travel-related purchases. Consumers are sought, screened, and seduced to buy in the effort to maximize spending.

But airports are not merely magnets for in-transit trade. Because they are entry and exit points they also act as virtual borders, even though they are not always at the geographical edge of the territory concerned. Thus they are also sites for security and surveillance practices and processes. If the airport check-in counter (or card-operated machine) is where ticket details are verified, the security, customs, and immigration stations are where travel documents, passports, and visas are scrutinized. Here, travelers are also screened for eligibility to travel and for acceptability on arrival. Or rather, this is where screening once took place.

After 9/11, the physical place of the border became even more delocalized (and detemporalized as well) in the sense that the processes traditionally carried out there were shifted back upstream. Identification checks and policing now take place prior to arrival. This is the "intelligent" border crossing. But, in addition, checks may also occur afterwards. The current Canadian plan, under the auspices of the Canada Customs and Revenue Agency, is to construct the Advance Passenger Information database to retain data on passengers for six years, including their destination, form of payment, and seat selection.[32] The idea of checking in at a specific time and at a specific place is giving way to an ongoing process of monitoring. As Mark Salter observes, this signals a shift in governmental policing, "from examination of travelers to the surveillance of the general mobile population."[33]

Surveillance occurs in two analytically separate contexts in airports: for maximal commerce and for national security. Consumer screening occurs through many means, at ticketing, in frequent flyer and air mile loyalty clubs, as well as in credit card, cell-phone, internet, and telephone use. Citizen screening occurs through machine-readable passports, x-ray machines, and, increasingly, various kinds of biometric devices for identification and checking. Surveillance screens and sorts personal data in order to classify consumers and citizens in terms of relative worth and relative risk. Many kinds of surveillance occur at airports, and although they are analytically separable into "citizen" and "consumer" domains, these are increasingly blurred.

This makes airports an interesting microcosm for considering what might be thought of as dual surveillance systems. They are characteristic of the kinds of monitoring, checking, tracking, and supervision that occur in the wider society. Over the past 20 years it has become increasingly clear that surveillance has spilled well over the containers of the nation-state and the capitalist enterprise, into every conceivable life-sphere – but especially down commercial conduits.[34] But many analysts argued and some still do – that commercial surveillance and state surveillance would maintain their distinct integrities. Surveillance would remain dual (or, maybe, multiple).

Other observers thought differently, arguing that new networked information systems produce not only the potential, but also certain strong incentives, to share personal data between and across different kinds of agency. Thus commercial agencies could be co-opted to provide assistance to the police, customs and immigration, or intelligence services. And data collected by state-sponsored or regulated agencies may in some circumstances be usable by commercial interests. What would simply not have been conceivable in the days of index cards and filing cabinets becomes a feasible and attractive proposition to both large organizations and high-technology companies. This is the age of the internet and of searchable databases, when speed and security are at a premium.

September 11, 2001 provided the opportunity for just such a convergence of hitherto (largely) parallel surveillance systems. Airports proved to be the obvious site for the most far-reaching experiments and policies for implementing networked surveillance in new integrated formats. Of course, this did not happen overnight. Limited modes of personal data exchange have existed for a long time, at airports as elsewhere. Does anyone still believe that the undulating, liquid, commercial surveillance assemblage is somehow innocent of state-sponsored social control? Or that "Big Brother" is no more than a mode of escapist television entertainment? Such naivety was exposed in the aftermath of 9/11.

Today, records of passenger transactions and movement proliferate and, as we shall see, cross-breed. Airlines and the airports that service them exist today under the sign of information. Finding out about travelers' patterns of spending, their preferred routes, and who will pay their bills is vital to the competitiveness of the airlines. This kind of marketing data has been sought with increasing intensity ever since airlines switched to fully computerized systems for ticketing. The advent of the searchable database is vital to such data-processing, because it permits matching and comparing records with unprecedented speed. In the 1980s, ticket reservation systems such as Sabre and Galileo appeared, immediately raising the competitive stakes just mentioned.[35]

When an airline ticket is purchased, a series of typical events follow.[36] A Passenger Name Record (PNR) is created within the Computerized Reservation System (CRS, a database headquartered in Europe). The PNR includes a name, itinerary, phone number, ticketing payment mode, and the name of the person making the reservation. To this is added the final price, and if payment is by credit card, its type, number, expiry date, and merchant authorization code. Medical or dietary needs may be added, too, plus special details such as unaccompanied minor, deportee, prisoner, or special needs passenger.[37] Authorized system users have access to this data, which is purged from the Departure Control System two hours after a flight has landed, and from the CRS two days later. The PNR is retained on a separate database for a further two years for management analysis. Frequent flyer club members, who expect a more personalized service, obtain it at the cost of parting with more personal data. This comprises a more complete passenger flight history, hotel reservation and car rental needs, frequent flyer points, and other information.

The upshot of these practices, as Colin Bennett argues, is that despite the various data-protection and privacy regimes that exist, "international airlines have considerable power over individuals through the personal information they collect, process and disseminate." This makes it possible for the international airline system to "work as a system of surveillance."[38] This system is globalized, such that sometimes sensitive personal data flows across national and organizational borders with unprecedented implications. The uses to which these personal data are put may expand in incremental and unplanned ways, and within a complex and non-transparent system at that.

Although the airline competition of the past two decades was the product of widespread deregulation, this does not mean that all regulations have vanished. The International Air Transport Association (IATA) and the influential Federal Aviation Authority (FAA) in the USA do have a considerable say over how airlines operate. The International Civil Aviation Organization writes the regulations for passports in the international realm.[39] In particular, rising demands have been made on ticketing and reservation systems to be available if required for legal and policing purposes.

In the late 1990s the Computer-Assisted Passenger Screening (CAPS) system was introduced by the FAA, which rates passengers according to 40 data items based on ticketing data. Some of the profiling standards are secret, and they permit certain passengers to be selected for increased scrutiny based on the number of hits, plus some further random searches.[40] The CAPS system, and its cognates elsewhere, provide the link between consumer and security surveillance. Today, the CAPS system has been vastly expanded, for reasons that are not hard to fathom. First, some background is needed to understand the genesis of security in the air.

Highjacking History

In 1971 one Dan Cooper boarded a plane in Portland Oregon, and during the flight passed a note to a cabin crew member to the effect that he was carrying a bomb. He demanded that the plane land to drop off passengers and to pick up a ransom and a parachute, which he would later take with him as he jumped out of the rear door of the aircraft. Technical modifications were made to the plane following this and other similar incidents, such as a "Cooper Vane" being fitted to prevent the rear door from being opened in flight.[41] Indeed, with each new hijack challenge has come some matching technical solution, that worked until overcome by further cleverness or audacity on the part of hijackers.

After a hijacker forced a plane to circle over a nuclear facility in Oak Ridge Tennessee in 1972, armed security personnel were placed at boarding checkpoints, and baggage was checked from 1973. Ground crews had to be checked from the mid-1980s after a TWA flight from Athens had weapons put in the washrooms by cleaners, and this was followed by bag-and-passenger matching before take-off. The Pan Am flight 103 that was brought down over Lockerbie, Scotland, had a bomb hidden in a radio, which prompted the use of CT scanners to obtain

3-D images of all bag contents. The number of hijacks has decreased as the technical hurdles have become higher, but the loss of life in each successive attack has increased.

Against this backdrop it is easy to see why the attacks on New York and Washington on September 11, 2001 would lead to such a massive call for increased high-technology security and surveillance. The cleverness of the plan, its neat timing for mass media coverage, its totally unanticipated scope, and the huge and tragic loss of life clearly called for commensurate response. No question, given the history of previous technical responses to hijacking, that the answer would have to involve far greater technological sophistication in the proffered solutions. No wonder that ideas that had been mooted before, but rejected on the grounds of prohibitive cost, or of threats to civil liberties, would now be considered as plausible options. In this climate, it would even be attractive to use data from CAPS to isolate profiles of likely suspects and subject them and their bags to extra pre-boarding scans.

In fact, exactly this strategy is now being pursued in the USA, in a long-term, multimillion-dollar scheme announced early in 2002, involving federal aviation authorities, airlines, and high-technology companies. If this scheme becomes fully operational as planned, every passenger without exception will be screened by an integrated system that will pull together travel histories and living arrangements, along with demographic and other personal information. Every reservation system in the USA will have networked links with private and government databases, and data-mining and predictive software will profile passenger activities to intuit any available clues about potential threats, before they have a chance to be realized.[42] This is anticipatory, pre-emptive, algorithmic surveillance of an advanced, sophisticated, and unprecedented kind.

Dancing Development

Technological development is not a relentless juggernaut. Rather, technical enhancements to security-related surveillance may be seen more as a successive dance, or fencing match, in which threats are met with increasingly sophisticated responses. As for the consumer surveillance at airports, this has followed a general pattern for the deployment of database marketing and "loyalty clubs" common to the "social management" practices that have characterized consumer capitalism more and more over the past 25 years. In each case, the exponential growth of airlines and airports in the same period has meant that both consumer and security surveillance systems have been large-scale ones. This in turn implies expensive infrastructural investments and surveillance systems that are unlikely to be dismantled in any hurry.

But developments in each sphere do not explain why these systems should converge, or why they would converge at a particular time. One area concerns the erection of technical obstacles and disincentives to violent or criminal activity on aircraft, which has shifted steadily toward the screening of travelers and their baggage. The other has to do with trying to retain customers and to induce others to fly with one airline rather than another, as well as with attempting to enhance the consumer experiences at any given airport. The logic of connecting a minimum of personal flight details relates to health and safety concerns, and to the convenience and efficiency of using airline personnel for tasks such as handing out boarding cards that are required by immigration and customs departments.

A telling technical logic for system integration began to appear in the 1980s, however, which is the development of searchable databases and, with the advent of serious networking, remotely searchable databases. It is not evidence of succumbing to technological determinism to observe that the kinds of system being proposed today, while technically conceivable, were simply not commercially available until a relatively few years ago. Now that they are available, though, many different kinds of operation may be undertaken using similar kinds of software (as we saw in chapter 4). The system of sorting by category is not only highly complex and based on powerful networked computers, it may be used for quite varied purposes. What Gary T. Marx dubbed "categorical suspicion" in policing contexts is little different in logic from the processes of "categorical seduction" which I argue is at the heart of contemporary consumer surveillance.[43]

During the same 30-year period, great strides have been made in the fields of data-protection and privacy regulation. The best of these rely upon widely acknowledged – if not universally respected – "fair information practices." These include principles such as that data collected for one purpose should not be used for another without the informed consent of data-subjects, and data pertaining to a person should be available to that person for checking, updating, and correcting. Although such regulation often leaves much to be desired, it nonetheless placed real limits on the promiscuous sharing, exchange, and sale of personal data and has discouraged those who would expand either policing or consumer surveillance systems on a just-in-case or an opportunistic basis. So while high-tech companies are enthusiastically conscious of the potential for systems integration, regulatory authorities and public opinion have inhibited such processes on civil liberties or "privacy" grounds.

9/11 proved to be the big event that catalyzed change. The balance shifted decisively from deliberate deafness to "integrated systems" siren calls from high-tech companies, to a willingness to countenance their possibility; from a sense that public opinion and civil rights group pressure would prevent massive data-sharing schemes, to the conviction that the attacks were of sufficient magnitude to warrant overriding accepted fair information practices; from relaxed attitudes to small items on aircraft that could be used as weapons and from a consumerist stress on the "fun" and "freedom" aspects of airport routines (with minimal but serious security checks), to vigilance about every knitting needle and plastic knife and the mounting of armed guards at gates and air marshals on flights.

The consequences of these shifts are likely to be far-reaching, and represent a major enhancement of the social power of information, especially in sorting and screening personal data.[44] Over the past few years surveillance systems in every sphere of life, and articulated with risk management,[45] have come to contribute significantly to the reproduction of social divisions. This is a process that is accelerating in the wake of September 11. While facial recognition technologies, "smart" identity cards, iris scans, hand scans, and gait recognition schemes all work using searchable databases to sift personal traits and traces, at airports these are likely to become adjuncts to a larger integrated system that will cover every single traveler in transit.

The systems being developed and tested in the USA during 2002 search for patterns of living arrangements, meetings, transactions, spending habits, behaviors, and lifestyle preferences to create a "threat index" for each passenger. Each of the prototype systems involves coordinating public and private records to create models of "normal" activity, from which aberrations may be gauged and monitored. Using neural network software and relational databases, every flight will have a prioritized passenger list showing the least to the greatest threats. Companies argue that the best results will be obtained using the greatest number of sources, from linking consumer with passport data, plus a national ID and a biometric identifier.

The system, known as CAPPS II, introduces the word "Pre-screening" into the title, thus joining several other initiatives that put the surveillance focus on the future, attempting to anticipate and thus to pre-empt attacks.[46] The mathematically derived "threat index" is produced by an application that analyzes data from the FBI, the National Crime Information Center (NCIC), State Department databases, Internal Revenue Service (IRS), Social Security Administration, state motor vehicle and corrections department, credit bureau, and bank records.[47] Here we see very clearly the convergence of different kinds of database into a system capable of cross-checking between government and commercial spheres, and in which "function creep" is facilitated by the fact that data-subjects themselves trigger updates, for instance by renewing licenses.

Already, Logan Airport in Boston has announced the installation of new scanners. They check the authenticity of hundreds of kinds of driver's license and passport, check the bearer's name against government "watch lists" and generate lists, with photos, of whose document was checked and when.[48] If all these schemes come to fruition, the merger of consumer and citizenship data will be complete, and the previously parallel lines will converge into an integrated system.

Toward Global Integration?

Four major implications of the post-September 11 convergence of dual surveillance systems may be highlighted as key areas for social analysis and political concern. Together, they might seem to be evidence for the global integration of at least one kind of surveillance, at airports. But while global integration may be the goal of some, it is unlikely that this will occur, at least in the short term.

The first implication is that the decisive tilt toward abstract algorithmic systems shifts surveillance methods even further away from labor-intensive and human-operated systems. Both algorithmic and non-algorithmic (such as CCTV using human operators) systems are discriminatory and tend towards exclusionary practices.[49] The impact of non-algorithmic systems is "moderated by the threefold interaction between the subjects, the technologies, and their human operators." In contrast, algorithmic systems "attempt to configure human behaviors remotely without the uncertainty provided by direct human operation."[50]

The dream of pre-emptive surveillance is perpetuated within such automated systems, even though past evidence suggests that net-widening produces only petty criminals rather than the ones the systems are designed to identify. At the same time, in Israel, where a personal interrogation and assessment of passengers – rather than reliance on a high-tech screening system – has been operated by El Al, a 30-year record of safety has been maintained.[51] Yet the social costs are huge; it is unlikely that the El Al system of negative discrimination against some groups would ever be acceptable in North America or Europe.

A second implication of converging (algorithmic) airport surveillance is that such systems tend to become increasingly opaque. This is because system designers and computer programmers play a greater role in creating the categories, which are the criteria for discrimination. In other words, the processes by which unusual or abnormal behaviors are defined are tasks for "technical experts" rather than ones in which there is ethical scrutiny or democratic involvement. Yet the categories comprising the "threat index" make all the difference to the chances of passengers flying freely, or being apprehended for further searches, questioning, and delays. As country of origin and ethnicity play a large part in these decisions, it would be unremarkable if the modes of discrimination actually followed familiar patterns, now reinforced by their high-technology gloss. So the question is unlikely to be whether or not such systems will be implemented, as whether adequate means of independent oversight and system accountability can be built into them.

A third, more general implication of the new airport surveillance is that air travel is becoming a much more intensive site for state control. To imagine that airline deregulation or economic globalization somehow means a diminution of national governmental involvement in the personal details of passengers is naive. True, in recent years the existence has become clear of a widespread, networked, surveillant assemblage, created by a plethora of agencies both public and private, commercial and legal. But what responses to September 11 show is that the state, so far from withering, is waxing strong in crucial contexts such as airports. Contemporary governments, notably in the US, are demonstrating their capacity to use, for very centralized ends, just those decentralized and dispersed monitoring and screening systems that are elsewhere viewed as harbingers of more benign, soft surveillance. National security is one such end, and, as Michael

Ignatieff points out, for the USA there remain global security obligations, too.[52]

The fourth implication of the convergence of dual surveillance systems is that airports, as key arenas of the "war on terrorism," are worth watching as possible microcosms of wider global and societal surveillance trends. As I noted earlier, the political economy of surveillance is crucial to such developments. Governments are putting huge resources into "counter-terrorism," and software companies are offering both their expertise and their products as solutions to the urgent question of security. These are the priorities that shape the algorithms that produce the socially sorted persons.

Few would be foolish enough to say that safety in the skies is not a priority. But equally, all too few seem wise enough to acknowledge that such safety should be sought in tandem with enhanced modes of public scrutiny over automated systems. Along with this would also come the recognition that sometimes those systems may be simply inferior to more labor-intensive ones. Without such cautions, the same political economy that frames airport surveillance will help shape security and policing arrangements in the world beyond the "non-places" of those transit areas, travelers' malls, check-ins, security stations, and gates.

Globalizing Counter-surveillance

The growth of global surveillance may be secretive but it has not gone unnoticed. It may seem like business as usual in newly developed and developing countries, but in the global north new surveillance practices have not all been greeted with gratitude. In many Asian and Middle Eastern countries, 9/11 served as a means of legitimizing already existing surveillance practices by governments that would be considered authoritarian or repressive in the West. Not much changed in Egypt, for example, where Islamists and the Muslim Brotherhood have been watched carefully for some time.

In South-East Asia, Indonesia, Singapore, and Malaysia in particular have used 9/11 as a reason for tightening controls, not least because al-Qaeda members have been active in each country. The Association of South-East Asian Nations (ASEAN) has agreed to deepen their countries' anti-terrorism cooperation[53] but because of the sanctions against political dissent in some of its member states it is difficult to know how far popular assent to this goes. Japan offers a more contradictory example, however. While the government has introduced several pieces of post-9/11 legislation – to identify customers' financial transactions and limiting the financing of "terrorist" groups – lawyers and academics have also spoken out collectively against the "globalization of law enforcement by international treaty."[54]

After 9/11, surveillance has moved more into public consciousness. Especially in the global north, this is being answered by a rapidly burgeoning network of surveillance critique and activism, both online and offline. Those already existing agencies dedicated to challenging increased surveillance, both statutory and grass roots, have hugely expanded their activities since 9/11. Privacy watchdogs and data-protection officials have voiced their concerns about the surveillance aspects of anti-terrorist legislation. Organizations such as Privacy International and the Electronic Privacy Information Center have posted online details of each apparent or potential abuse as well as of each proposed and actual new system.

These organizations have also hosted seminars and press conferences, while in other places, quite new groups

have sprung into being, stung by the enormity of surveillance challenges arising since 9/11. In Australia, for
instance, lively public meetings were held in Sydney and
Melbourne in 2002 under the title "City-State," to document and raise awareness of the surveillance consequences
of anti-terrorist initiatives in that country.[55] In several
European countries, questions are being raised about the
type and extent of post-9/11 measures by security, policing, and intelligence agencies. Identity card proposals, in
particular, have come in for considerable critique in some
countries. It would be surprising if at least some of this
activity were not translated into policy or more systematic
resistance.

As with the globalizing of surveillance itself, responses
have been globalizing for some time. Privacy International
(PI), for example, documents the growth of surveillance
systems and practices throughout the world. And it does
so using the internet, thus making publicly available to
many, and in many countries, the results of its surveys
and studies. Privacy International, based in London, England, and in Washington DC, helps to inform groups that
often work remotely from each other, enabling their activities to be coordinated and publicized very rapidly around
the world. PI may thus be thought of as a limited example
of globalized counter-surveillance. It does report on
countries around the world, especially in Asia, even
though most of its activities are in Europe and North
America. Similar activities are undertaken by the Electronic Privacy Information Center (EPIC) and the Global
Internet Liberty Campaign (GILC).

At the level of privacy and data-protection law, activities have been globalized for a number of years. Indeed,
the very designations, "privacy" and "data-protection,"
hint at alternative legal ways of conceiving the issues raised
by surveillance. The former is most frequently used in

North America, while various kinds of "data-protection" regimes exist in Europe.[56] Since the 1980s, if not before, however, European initiatives have had an influence on what happens in North America, and this is especially true of the "Data Protection Directive" that appeared in the early 1990s and came into force later in that decade. It requires trading partners to comply with certain standards of fair information practices, and this has served as a globalizing dynamic that attempts to limit the growth of some aspects of surveillance. The USA and Canada have both introduced legislation prompted by the European Directive.[57]

The long-term effectiveness of globalized groups that use the internet for communication and coordination has yet to be seen. But it does seem significant that the growth of globalized challenges and perceived threats is being met in this globalized way. It is an example of what Naomi Klein describes as a kind of "hotlink" politics, where hierarchy is bypassed by a decentralized movement, and in which new technologies take on an almost subversive character.[58] Of course, she is also well aware of the dangers of this approach. A mere web-surfing armchair activism may also result, for instance. But it is clear from numerous studies that such "downsides" are just that. The internet is being shaped by many as a means of seeking justice, locally and globally, and its capacity to do so is already becoming apparent.[59]

Global Surveillance?

The result of globalized surveillance is not global surveillance. Fears of some wired world government controlling the global masses through a unified panoply of surveillance technologies is a far-fetched paranoid nightmare.

But what is increasingly in evidence is a worldwide network of surveillance that is capable of integrating personal data-processing systems, using multiple sources, public and private, to do so. The global north is currently where most integration occurs, but there is growing cooperation between it and some specific states in other regions. Policing is increasingly globalized, as is intelligence-gathering. The networks that enable this are both elastic in space, stretched over vast distances, and pulled taut in time, drawing together very quickly the results of searches in integrated databases.

More groups are drawn into the surveillance net, and these groups have similar characteristics as sprawling definitional categories (such as "terrorist") and similar search methods are used to identify, screen, and sort them. Certainly, it seems that the economic and military power of the global north can only be augmented through the use of such systems, but it is also the power of certain groups that is reinforced. The "new economy" theorists and politicians who essentially see globalization as a "good thing" are almost bound to view any species of "anti-globalization" movement in a negative light. Thus members of the latter movements find themselves labeled as "potential terrorists," just because they dissent from received wisdom and economic "common sense."

But just as there are anti-globalization movements, so there are anti-surveillance movements, at least in embryonic form, operating globally. It would appear that the kinds of "dialectic of control" common to modern times are being reshaped for global ones. Whereas, once, oppositional movements arose in response to capitalist control (labor unions) or industrial organization (green movements) within specific nation-states, now globalized forms of protest, action, and policy-formation are appearing as countervailing forces to globalizing processes such as surveillance. The networking style that facilitates integrated real-time surveillance also enables the "hotlink politics" that uses the internet to raise awareness and to coordinate action at a distance.

6

Resisting Surveillance

"I don't want to live in a country where people deceive each other, where people look at each other as if they were potential terrorists . . . I want to live in a country in which one can and does assume helpfulness and cooperation."

Ursula Franklin[1]

The surveillance consequences of 9/11 provide an opportunity to rethink surveillance and also, I believe, to resist it. Thus far, already existing systems have been reinforced, increasing the tendency for cultures of control and of suspicion to be augmented. At least some of the intended outcomes of intensified surveillance are unlikely to be realized, whereas the unintended consequences are already appearing.

In the past few years, surveillance has become algorithmic, technological, pre-emptive, and classificatory, in every way broadening and tightening the net of social control and subtly stretching the categories of suspicion. It thus tends to undermine trust and, through its emphasis on individual behaviors, to undermine social solidarity as well. At the same time, it augments the power of those who institute such systems, without increasing their accountability. All these features have been amplified since 9/11.

Several years ago, when I first started researching and writing about surveillance, I endeavored to maintain an appropriate stance that was neither paranoid nor complacent. I argued (and still do) that surveillance of some kind is both socially necessary and desirable but that it is always ambiguous. The dangers and risks attending surveillance are as significant as its benefits. In contexts where I felt people were being alarmist and shrill I cautioned restraint and pleaded for more careful analysis. In contexts where complacency seemed to reign I tried to show that surveillance has real effects on people's life-chances and life-choices that can at times be very negative.

Since 9/11, however, the pendulum has swung so wildly from "care" to "control" that I feel compelled to turn more robustly to critique. While I still insist that attitudes to surveillance should be ambivalent, the evidence discussed in this book obliges me to observe that oblique dissent will no longer do. Some instances of early twenty-first-century surveillance are downright unacceptable, as they directly impugn social justice and human personhood. They help to create a world where no one can trust a neighbor, and where decisions affecting people and polity are made behind closed doors or within "smart" systems.

This is not merely a negative critique, however. Major challenges confront the world following 9/11. There is a need for positive suggestions about other ways forward. The challenges, I suggest, are analytical, political, and technological. That is, the challenges affect how the social world after 9/11 is understood; how it is ethically judged and what are taken to be priorities for action; and how people might participate in deciding what technologies are adopted. The world is even more complex, unstable, and risky after 9/11. But those are reasons for engagement with it, not withdrawal.

Drawing Threads Together

Surveillance as a central social process was already highly developed in most countries of the world before September 11, 2001. Modern societies are surveillance societies, even before they depend on digital technologies, but more fully so after computerization. Surveillance practices and processes were already being augmented by networked communication systems before 9/11, and change was accelerating. More and more surveillance cameras were being installed in urban areas, for example, not only in Britain and other European countries, but in North America and Asia as well. In many ways, however, the effect of 9/11 has been to accelerate the adoption of surveillance practices, such as Neighborhood Watch informers, and technologies, such as internet tracking. The attacks triggered intensified surveillance in many spheres.

Current evidence suggests that already existing trends in contemporary society are being reinforced since 9/11, especially the cultures of fear, control, suspicion, and secrecy. The first, fear, is easily amplified by the mass media, which was clearly seen just after 9/11 itself. The "irrational" attacks, apparently "from outside," mean that "no one is safe." The endless replays of WTC footage themselves helped foster fear and eroded resistance to new surveillance regimes. The second, control, as David Garland has eloquently argued, is not a conspiracy of the powerful.[2] Rather, those in power have capitalized on certain social developments, especially the rise of the consumer-citizen and of privatized mobility, to institute forms of commodified control. These depend on calcu-

lating risks and on seeking information through surveillance.

The culture of suspicion follows from the first two. It is
a consequence of dependence on a multitude of tokens of
trust rather than on direct relations of trust, and of course
it has been exacerbated by 9/11. The fear produced by the
New York attacks, as Onora O'Neill argues, undermines
trust in a peculiarly vicious way.³ Finally, the culture of
secrecy has always been a temptation of bureaucratic
departments and governments, and it flies in the face of
democratic practices. It too has mushroomed since 9/11.

Irony repeatedly rears its head in this book. The laws
passed in the wake of 9/11 often cover ground already
covered by existing law, are unlikely to succeed in their
stated aims of making terrorist attacks less likely, but are
highly likely to have effects not explicitly intended by
them. Similarly with new technological measures geared
to minimizing risks of repeat attacks. Many are poorly
suited to their purposes, while being lamentably conducive
to other consequences. Of course, it is understandable
that emergency powers, quickly-passed legislation, and
hurriedly-installed technologies will have flaws, but the
ironies of initiatives following 9/11 go beyond these. They
hint at a lack of understanding of actual situations (how
devious intelligent terrorist plotters are likely to be, or why
networked attacks are not amenable to conventional centralized responses, for example). And they rely on time-
honored solutions, technical fixes, and tighter controls,
applied across the board.

Surveillance trends have solidified after September 11,
especially those of social sorting. The much-publicized
debates over "racial profiling" places this in high relief,
but the issues are broader than this. Negative discrimination toward those defined as "Muslim/Arabs" is certainly
occurring. This is one of the most insidious results of

9/11, not least because it connects suspicions with particular ethnic and religious groups regardless of on-the-ground realities. But social sorting is even more evident than before as a foreground feature of surveillance. All kinds of group may be included in the "terrorist" category, and all kinds of activity, including casual chat, may be construed as suspicious. Such classification frequently takes place using human observers, but it becomes far more powerful when computer-assisted.

Other surveillance trends have also been accented since 9/11. One is the trend towards system integration. This is a goal that has long been shared by both technical system designers and by organization managers. The principle permits data – in this case personal data – to be shared across a range of departments or sections that today are typically networked. Searches and retrieval from remote sites are relatively straightforward. System integration always militates against the principles of fair information handling. This is because such principles create friction in the system, slowing down disparate record linkages and refusing access to certain data. Yet integration performs many functions of centralization, such that power may in fact be more concentrated, even though it appears geographically to be dispersed. The so-called surveillance assemblage, which loosely links numerous data-sets and sources of information, may not itself be hierarchical, but this does not mean that power-pyramids are a thing of the past.

Last but not least, surveillance is being effectively globalized, a process that has been gathering speed since September 11. Personal data of all kinds are flowing more freely across borders, between airport authorities and police and intelligence agencies in the global north in particular. Already flowing data – especially via the internet – are subject to more and more checks and monitors.

But if globalization originates in that very modern process of doing things at a distance, then it is clear that surveillance was set to be globalized from the start. The focused attention on personal details for management and control which comprises surveillance stretches increasingly over time and space, courtesy of new communication technologies. In terms of everyday practices, this touches directly on the "delocalized border." New measures move the information search away from the literal border as surveillance is globalized.

A further irony is this. The globalization processes that enabled the attacks of 9/11 to take place also enable efforts to apprehend potential terrorists. But in addition, they allow others to share information about negative aspects of surveillance and to warn others that not only the twin towers, but the towers of democratic involvement may also now be tumbling.

At the outset, I tried to show how surveillance responses to 9/11 are a lens for seeing two kinds of phenomenon: what is already happening and what is likely to happen in the future. It is important to step back again and recall that much of what has been brought forward as security-through-surveillance was already present in the policing, administrative, and consumer systems of countries around the world, but especially in the global north. 9/11 prompted an acceleration and an intensification of shifts toward surveillance societies that were already very visible in social life. Scholars, film-makers, artists, and political activists were already seeking to show that some trends were more than a minor cause for concern. Even without 9/11, surveillance trends were emerging as a contested site, despite the fact that they had few political champions.

The lens of 9/11 responses also helps us see what sorts of direction are taken when states of emergency are declared and panic regimes take over. As we start to focus on this aspect of surveillance, some things seem scarcely credible. Certainly they appear contradictory. In the USA especially, the rush toward tight control appears to be reminiscent of highly authoritarian regimes of which the USA has been highly critical in the past. And the relentless hunt for enemies within is uncannily like that which occurred during the McCarthy era, only now "terrorists" with particular ethnic backgrounds rather than "communists" with particular national sympathies are the target. When surveillance turns ordinary citizens into suspects it is time for serious stocktaking.

Such social self-examination seems appropriate in the light of the apocalyptic aspects of 9/11 and the surveillance that is being established in its wake. Responses to 9/11 disclose already existing trends and simultaneously hint at a reckoning, a judgment. Normative approaches, already implicitly present in analysis and theory, need to be highlighted. It is one thing to be made aware of situations where freedoms are being constrained, human rights neglected, and people are suffering needlessly for things they have not done and for deeds they never contemplated; it is another to suggest what to look out for as warning signs as new measures are proposed, what sorts of alternative are appropriate, and why some kinds of response are preferable to others.

Meeting the Challenges

Three major challenges confront those who would resist the surveillance consequences of September 11: grasping their social, political, and technological dimensions. By the first I refer especially to analysis done in the social sciences. Secondly, there are pressing ethical choices in a world where the politics of information are moving to center stage. And thirdly, understanding the technological dimensions of surveillance, especially after 9/11, is vital to any appraisal of what is going on in the world of identifying, locating, monitoring, tracking, and managing individuals and groups.

The Social Question

September 11, 2001 did not create the need for fresh concepts and new explanatory tools, but it does show how urgently they are needed now. Surveillance has to be understood today as social sorting, which has exclusionary consequences. Watching others has become systematic, embedded in a system that classifies according to certain pre-set criteria, and sorts into categories of risk or opportunity. These categories relate in turn to suspicion or to solicitation – and many others in between – depending on the purposes for which the surveillance is done. Such classification is very important to people's life-chances (as Max Weber would have put it) and choices. Surveillance is becoming a means of placing people in new, flexible, social classes.

How persons are "made up" by surveillance systems, and with what consequences, is a vital question. If the "data double"[4] that circulates through electronic systems does help to determine what sorts of treatment we receive from insurance companies, the police, welfare departments, employers, or marketing firms, then it is far from an innocent series of electronic signals. This is acutely true if ethnic, religious, or other contentious characteristics help comprise that data image. It also means that understanding how the coding systems work is also of utmost importance.

Struggles over classification are not new. What is new today is that classification processes are being automated, and used for a wide variety of tasks within increasingly dominant modes of risk management. Power over classificatory schemes, as Pierre Bourdieu argues, is central to the meaning of the social world. Law contributes to the codifying of classifications, as we saw with regard to definitions of terrorism. But technology buttresses this by removing further the human element, and by digitally facilitating the power of separation. Law and technology may seem remote to many, but their effects are felt locally, relationally, personally. As Bourdieu says: "The fate of groups is bound up with the words that designate them."[5] This could hardly be more true than for those today who are viewed first as "Arabs," "Muslims," or "terrorists." Surveillance practices enable fresh forms of exclusion that not only cut off certain targeted groups from social participation, but do so in subtle ways that are sometimes scarcely visible. Indeed, the automating of surveillance permits a distance to be maintained between those who are privileged and those who are poor, those who are "safe" and those who are "suspect." This may be exclusion as domination, where the categories of outcast reflect deep and long-term tensions. But it may also be exclusion as abandonment in which the way is eased for some simply to "walk by on the other side."[6] So-called social defense technologies work the same way to keep out the proscribed persons as "fast-track" "preferred customer" technologies work to protect privilege.

This is a different kind of argument than is often made about surveillance. Especially in the USA, surveillance is often thought to be a threat to privacy. Editorial writers and activists complain about initiatives such as DARPA's Total Information Awareness as "supersnoop" schemes that imperil personal freedoms.[7] But this is to misconstrue and underestimate the power of surveillance. To think of surveillance primarily as endangering personal spaces of freedom is highly individualistic. It also misses the point about surveillance contributing to social sorting mechanisms. To process personal data in order to classify groups is to affect profoundly their choices and their chances in life. This is why the *social* analysis of surveillance is so essential to a proper understanding. And it is even more vital after 9/11.

Although 9/11 has brought some questions to the fore, in the twenty-first century surveillance affects everyone all the time. Its intensity varies from country to country and from agency to agency but it is increasingly generalized. In the global north in particular, risk management regimes rely on surveillance for their ongoing data-processing. The addition of "terrorist" categories to those already in operation dramatically deflects attention away from the routine and mundane operation of such systems. For most people, most of the time, insecurity and risk have precious little to do with anything as terrifying as terrorism. In homes and local communities it is items like the vagaries of the job market, the burden of debt, and the fracturing of relationships that constitute risk. Single mothers suspected of welfare fraud also have much to fear. For governments seeking to distract concern over poverty and inequality in their own countries and abroad, anti-terrorist surveillance provides an excellent decoy.

Another important caution: surveillance is not merely about new technologies. Ordinary people play a role within the surveillance process. The power of surveillance varies with circumstances, with the knowledge of the system held by its subjects, and with the responses that people make to the fact of being under surveillance. Sociologically, much power relates to economic factors; the rich tend to rule. Other aspects of power relate to status, to groups active in their pursuit of political goals, or to personal information held by those who have access to it. Power is always a social relationship, and it is always contested or contestable.

But power is also a resource. The more that power relates to data – retrievable information about groups and individuals that can be cross-checked to filter out particular persons – the more surveillance becomes, in principle, a political matter. If Anthony Giddens is correct, a "dialectic of control" tends to emerge in relation to each of the key axes of power that have developed in the modern world.[8] If surveillance is becoming a central such axis, then what kinds of opposition to its negative features can be anticipated or encouraged? I shall return to this issue in a moment, when we look at the political challenge.

Compliance with surveillance is commonplace. Most of the time, and for many reasons, people go along with surveillance. It is a taken-for-granted fact of the modern world that we have to give our PIN at the bank machine, our driver's license to police, our health card number at the hospital. We assume that our employer, telephone company, and frequent flyer club will have a number for our records, and that when we vote in national or municipal elections our names will be listed. We assume that the benefits – security, efficiency, safety, rewards, convenience – are worth the price of having our personal data recorded, stored, retrieved, cross-checked, traded, and exchanged in surveillance systems. As ordinary subjects go along with surveillance, so the order constructed by the system is reinforced, and persons are "normalized" (as Foucault would say) by the system. Since September 11, compliance has been even more marked, for many, with the additional "fear factor." At the same time, as we shall see, challenges have also appeared, the long-term consequences of which have yet to be seen.

Compliance may not be unwitting, as is seen from the many examples of negotiating surveillance that occur from day to day. Although as yet social scientists know all too little about how people respond to being constant subjects of surveillance, some examples of negotiating it may be mentioned. Subjects may confound the categories when they do not recognize themselves in the descriptions of any number of questionnaires. Teenagers may play up to or evade the cameras in the shopping mall. People required to go through a "routine check" ordeal may refuse – "I ain't going to pee in no jar."[9] Employees may draw the line at public displays of keystrokes or at cameras in canteens or washrooms. Consumers may find technical means of preventing spam arriving in the email inbox. In each case, it may not be that the whole surveillance system is in question, but rather that some aspect of it is challenged.

In some of the above cases, questioning surveillance is just an individual matter, whereas in others, groups may be collectively involved. Individual refusals do count, but when groups and movements emerge that are committed to resisting surveillance or some aspects of it, then counter-surveillance becomes a more serious social phenomenon. Over the past couple of decades, a number of groups have appeared that make it their business to challenge the power of surveillance, most often in the name of privacy or of civil rights. Some issues have become *causes célèbres*, such as the proposal to create a "Clipper Chip" that would give a key to government to unlock encryption codes,[10] or the outcry against Lotus "Household Marketplace" software that would have made personal data by zipcodes available for sale on a massive scale.[11] Note that both these occurred in the USA, and both several years before 9/11. What has happened since builds on those precedents.

There is another, deeper, reason for questioning surveillance, however. The kinds of question just addressed tend to assume that because technological surveillance is growing, it is on these terms that it should be countered. But this is to accept the increasingly dominant terms of reference rather than doubting that discourse itself. This book has shown how in fact new technologies are socially embedded in the practices of institutional and everyday life. From executive decisions made in DARPA to mundane choices about whether to use a credit card or cash, a cellphone call or an email, the socio-technical is always in view. Or should be. We have also seen how the technological "solutions" tend to be self-augmenting and to be presented as the obvious ones. They have a rachet effect in which more systems breed more insecurity which creates a new need for more systems. And all too easily they seem to insinuate themselves into a monopoly position.

This cyclops vision is desperately deficient. So-called social defense technologies and situational crime prevention that have been proliferating over the past 30 years, and which now appear to many as the only viable solution to terrorism, are socially regressive. They tend to reinforce social divisions through social sorting, remove questions of moral responsibility by reducing the real issues to risk and containment, and render true debate a non-starter. This is why I have also stressed the need to consider not just the instrumental, but also the dimension of social life that we might call solidarities. Deeper than law and technology is the level of mutual recognition, of willingness to discuss, of social trust. Questions of surveillance – like those of technology in general or of globalization – can seem very remote even though in fact they affect ordinary lives intimately. An ethics of care for the Other that extends to the practical welcoming of strangers, a nurturing of small-scale communities of many kinds that can mediate between the large scale and the everyday, and a fostering of trust in appropriate ways – these are the soil within which such solidarities can grow. Whatever might be said about resisting surveillance, it is at this basic level that the practical task takes off.

Engaging a New Politics

The political challenge connects with the social analytical challenge, and indeed flows out of it. It has many aspects, and here I touch on just three. The first is the basic political challenge presented by the surveillance aspects of responses to 9/11. The idea of free democratic participation in an open society is under assault. The second has to do with the "dialectic of control" and raises the question of where leadership will come from in mitigating and reshaping surveillance practices. The third concerns the "politics of the code." This is a key aspect of politics in the twenty-first century, centering on the power of information and communication.

Whether seen in the lack of due process, the closed-door decisions of judges and politicians, the tendentious definitions of "terrorist," or the sheer authoritarianism of administrations engaged in the war on terrorism, democracy is in trouble after 9/11. Treating ordinary citizens as suspects, and simultaneously inciting them to spy on their neighbors, is an unlikely recipe for confidence in the political process. Placing security and military concerns at the top of the political agenda necessarily displaces freedom and democracy. They cannot coexist as equal priorities, at least under the current "surveillance state" regimes that are emerging. The attempt to tighten border security to keep out all manner of aliens may effectively close the door on the real needs of both the world outside and the world within.

Ulrich Beck notes the entrenchment of surveillance states after 9/11 but, like several others, he also advances an alternative: cosmopolitan states. These are characterized by solidarity, with foreigners inside and outside national borders. They would connect self-determination with responsibility for national and non-national Others. Thus: "Cosmopolitan states struggle not only against terror, but against the *causes* of terror."[12] This would lay the groundwork, Beck argues, for international cooperation on the basis of human rights and global justice. He does not discount or underplay the analysis of world risk society, for which he is justly famous. He insists rather that cosmopolitanism would be a way of civilizing it. This is an example of the road not (yet) taken as an alternative to the anti-democratic reinforcement of the surveillance state.

The revitalizing of the state is one challenge presented by the current dangerous drift towards surveillance states. Another is to discover what coalition of groups could tame existing surveillance power. If labor movements arose against the power of capitalist corporations, feminist movements against modern forms of patriarchy, and green movements against industrialism, then what countervailing movements arise against surveillance? It seems fair to argue that the activities of a range of social movements, dedicated to questioning surveillance excesses (which may in some case be surveillance per se) could count as actors in the dialectic of control now forming a firm shadow to surveillance activities in many contexts.

Since September 11, the kinds of agency, group, and movement that already challenged surveillance have redoubled their efforts. Recognizing that 9/11 provides new rationales for surveillance, along with a climate of fear and uncertainty, civil liberties groups and privacy commissions have been active in their critique and opposition to practices and technologies arising as a result of the attacks. Thus the Electronic Privacy Information Center (EPIC) and the American Civil Liberties Union (ACLU) have been prominent in voicing their unhappiness with new measures,[13] as have similar groups in other countries. Privacy International continues its invaluable work of documenting the growth of surveillance around the world, and of using Greenpeace-type publicity stunts to draw attention to the most blatant abuses. Liberty, in the UK, and Statewatch, in Europe more generally, play a cognate role. Also, government bodies that oversee data-protection and privacy have an important role. For instance, George Radwanski, the federal Privacy Commissioner of Canada, has been outspoken in his criticisms of the anti-terrorism law, as well as of matters like CCTV surveillance in Canadian cities – also growing since 9/11.

It is no accident that the activities of these groups have been strongly augmented since 9/11. In many countries surveillance has been intensified in the quest for security – but also in line with previous policy goals. So while Statewatch has appeared as a voice of dissent in Europe, other groups such as the Japanese Network Against Surveillance Technology (NAST) and the nascent Australian "City-State" activities, have been formed to unite opposition to post-9/11 surveillance developments. It is particularly interesting to note the rising disquiet about surveillance in Japan. Although not directly related to post-9/11 developments, major protests and uncharacteristic civil disobedience followed the introduction of the national computerized registry of citizens in 2002. Yokohama City declared that it would only support a voluntary registry, while Kokubunji simply refused to cooperate. They held a "disconnecting ceremony."[14] Even in the USA, where for a while it appeared that emotional responses would drown dissent, several cities – including

Berkeley, Cambridge, and Ann Arbor – have voted to defy
the PATRIOT Act. It is significant how much may be
achieved at a local level. Civil society and informal associations are an important alternative to the remoteness of
rationalized risk societies.

The same kinds of technology that enable remote networked surveillance are also used to enable communication between those who dissent, above all using the
internet. The groups mentioned above, which usually
work both online and offline, are all attempting to use
whatever means are at their disposal to open up public
spaces. This is in sharp contrast with the efforts to close
communication channels, and to envelop all significant
decisions in a fog of secrecy. Such public spaces, to which
democratic use of the internet is making important contri-
butions, are crucial to any return to democratic practice
after 9/11.

As the consequences of contemporary surveillance systems and of the specific fallout from 9/11 become clear,
so it is likely that more attention will be focused on the
code. As more systems are algorithmic, automating the
social sorting processes, so awareness of the crucial role of
software protocols is likely to rise. Ordinary people are,
not unsurprisingly, interested in how facial recognition or
racial profiling systems work. As Lawrence Lessig
observes, cyberspace is already ruled by the law of the
"code;" it never was the realm of unrestricted freedom
that some of its idealists imagined.[15] However arcane
technical software codes may appear, they are never neu-
tral, never innocent. They refer to the desires and purposes of those designing and implementing the systems,
and will express their categories. And, as Lucy Suchman
reminds us, categories have politics.[16]

Technological Citizenship

The third major challenge confronting all who are concerned about surveillance, especially after 9/11, is technological. Remember, doing technology is not a foolish error. As I understand it, technology is part of the human calling to use wisely and fairly the earth's resources. Surveillance technologies themselves fall within this rubric as long as a just and appropriate balance is maintained between care and control.

The technology challenge has several aspects to it. At the most immediate level, those involved directly in technological efforts to combat terrorism – and any other perceived evil – have to confront the old conundrum of the likely effects of their work. It is a conundrum because until some system is installed and working at least some of its effects are unknown. But after it is installed, it may be too late to undo any potential damage. What is needed at this level is a keen awareness of the likely consequences, such that limiting measures can be built into the system. Groups such as Computer Professionals for Social Responsibility have been cognizant of these issues for some time. When social sorting is central to surveillance, the dangers of unfair treatment and prejudicial categorization should be highlighted so that potential damage can be minimized.

Beyond this, a time may yet come when the response to new surveillance proposals has, simply, to be negative – don't do it! For many reasons explored in this book, the creation of new surveillance systems may be looked at skeptically. Missing the mark of networked terrorism, the possibilities of abuse, the likelihood of reinforcing social inequalities, the distraction from more appropriate responses – all these and more are good grounds for caution. But when powerful corporations are working with powerful government departments, and where there is public fear and political resort to fixes, those who speak for technological caution are likely to be voices crying in the wilderness. And yet in times like these it is precisely such voices that are needed.

At an even deeper level, it has to be acknowledged that the technological challenge is no longer merely one for technologists or for politicians to confront. It is not only that these matters are too important to be left to those people alone, but also that the challenge of technology is now one that involves everyone, in the intimate routines of everyday life. The development of technological citizenship[17] is called for, where the responsibilities and the privileges – and perhaps rights – associated with living in a world suffused with technology are a matter for ethical reflection and political practice. Such a process, if it is to succeed, will require some fundamental shifts in thinking.

The countries of the global north, especially the USA, are currently falling over themselves to pass laws and install technologies of mistrust. The cultures of suspicion and control are being legislated and automated. The notion of unreasonable search is blowing in the winds of change as single warrants now permit searches with few limits, online or offline, under the US PATRIOT Act. What would alternatives look like? Langdon Winner suggests that "designing technical systems that are loosely coupled and forgiving, structured in ways that make disruptions easily borne, quickly repaired,"[18] makes a lot of sense. He goes on to list local, renewable energy resources, rather than global ones that are always at risk, technologies operated locally by people who are known personally, and reducing dependence on risk-laden powers wrested from nature as parallel ways forward. Together, they add up to ways of "living lightly on the earth with justice and compassion," which would also help eliminate grievances that lie behind terrorist attacks.

If such proposals are to have any effect, those of us influenced by western ways will have to turn our backs decisively on the modern instrumental approach to technology. It will have to be exchanged for a more hermeneutical understanding. In the latter view, technologies are "forms of life," embedded in social practices, such that contexts and functions of technology are in constant interplay.[19] Our radical dependence on technology, at least in the global north, means that doing technology has to be seen as part and parcel of all the activities of everyday life. This includes professional, domestic, commercial, legal, and, of course, political life.

To bring this back to earth, the next step is to ask whether technology is serving democratically defined goals or undermining them. Or are technologies simply being removed from public oversight? Who is actually accountable for surveillance systems, and what are the democratic processes that establish this? Who decides on the categories? Such matters may be worked out at very local levels, via what are sometimes called "privacy audits" in universities, firms, or government departments. Beyond this, technological citizenship demands not only a concern with limiting and regulating technologies – especially surveillance technologies in this case – but also in designing new systems. So-called privacy-enhancing technologies have a role to play here.

The question of technology is also a challenge that, at least in the West, confronts some profound cultural claims about the power of technology. David Noble, for example, argues that a deep-seated religious project is expressed – notably in the USA – of transcendence through technology.[20] James Carey calls it the "technological sublime,"[21] the dream of a world perfected through technology, especially information and communication technologies. To resist technological developments, then, may be, to some, tantamount to sacrilege or blasphemy. When the technicist approach is privileged, questioning it seems quirky if not perverse. It is the voices of prophets that cry in the wilderness, witnessing to the state of the world and to the light of another way. And prophets often get silenced.

Beyond Suspicion and Secrecy

Surveillance after September 11 threatens to widen the net of suspicion and to deepen the darkness of secrecy. In the name of "security" and "risk" all manner of practices and processes are set in train that serve to obscure what is really going on. Questions of power are thus occluded, especially the power of some to classify others and to single them out for special treatment or for exclusion. In the twenty-first century, official classifications were already likely to become a central sociological concern, given their importance for the distribution of resources and benefits.[22] The categories of suspicion were but one means of classification before 9/11, but their range is now rapidly growing.

As for secrecy, it is being explicitly established again as a modus vivendi in the interests of a "war against terrorism." But it is also an effect of using certain technologies which render decisions – especially classificatory decisions – less visible. The first is intended, the second is not, or at least less obviously so. At least some risk of corruption and irrationality is present when power is wielded under cover of secrecy, and, as Sissela Bok argues, such secrecy feeds on itself.[23] It increases power without increasing accountability, but often requires more secrecy as greater power accumulates. As for the digital aspects of secrecy, what I have in mind is the ways in which automation tends to make systems opaque, especially to those most affected by them.

These cultures of suspicion and of secrecy are anti-ethical and anti-political. Their combined effect is to inhibit trust and to close down discussion. The reduction of key challenges to risk management and security means that risk profiles are applied to relationships, institutions, and places, and, wherever possible, to automate responses.[24] This is why such a heavy emphasis is being placed on border controls and identity documents including smart cards. But this removes any concerns with social and legal contexts, with questions of jurisdiction and power, and the complex reasons individuals and groups might have for crossing borders. It also has implications for specific countries. In the case of the American proposal for "perimeter continental security" US–Canadian relationships would change significantly if common entry and exit policies were established.[25]

Unfortunately, trends towards risk management and related security and surveillance practices were already emerging before 9/11. They have been bolstered all the more unquestioningly since. The subtle but serious processes of social classification carry with them real "risks" that are rendered invisible and irrelevant when the language of risk management is dominant. The supposedly scientific basis of risk management lends it credibility but strips it of meanings that matter to most people – that they are embodied persons who inhabit specific places. Modes of categorizing that pay little or no attention to actual persons and places may seem innocent but in fact have consequences for those people and those places. Yet because the workings of those processes are often beyond the reach of those ordinary people, they remain in relatively unaccountable spaces of bureaucracy or technology.

Responses to "terrorism" may all too easily give rise to totalitarian tendencies which, as Hannah Arendt astutely pointed out, are ultimately about terror.[26] I am not suggesting that current policies in any countries affected by the anti-terrorist rhetoric are themselves based on terror.[27] Arendt herself was concerned with the seeds and germs of twentieth-century totalitarianism. She held that they had much to do with belief in self-serving myths. Today, there are myths in abundance, such as guaranteed security or risk-proof surveillance, which are used to justify unfair and unaccountable policies. But Arendt's work is relevant in another way too. As Craig Calhoun reminds us, Arendt saw totalitarianism working directly on and within the private lives of families and individuals, which modern form of power Foucault has taught us so much about.[28] Translated into today's surveillance practices, the dangers are palpable.

It is in the mundane routines of everyday life that the effects, the dangers, of surveillance appear. Surveillance after 9/11 raises questions for all of us. Or rather, it prompts questions that ought to be asked. What kind of world do we want to live in? Fortress America? Maximum Security Europe? In early 2003 the burning question was, should the US and her allies attack Iraq to oust Saddam Hussein? But just as the war on terror is fought on more than one front, so too ordinary citizens should ask themselves, do we support the "war" in the "homelands"? If not, why not request or promote alternative approaches to security than those that simply stretch the net of suspicion, further foster the mood of fear, entrench the culture of control, and commodify dubious surveillance technologies as their antidotes?

Opposition to the gratuitous security-and-surveillance

aspects of the "war on terror" is required on many levels. Those who worry about privacy should not be discouraged from querying intensified surveillance. But they would also do well to move beyond the rampant individualism that perceives only "snoops" to consider the serious social consequences of the "sorters" who categorize and profile, to assess and influence people's life-chances. Those who deplore the spread of suspicion in employment, education, and other spheres could do more than merely wring their hands. Opportunities abound to show solidarity, to welcome stigmatized groups – such as Arab Muslims – and generally to trigger trust rather than fomenting fear.

Many people do have opportunities to let contrary opinions be heard about new technologies, just as views on unnecessary or unfair laws can be expressed in messages to papers or politicians. Why are those video cameras needed on the school bus? Why should government databases contain personal information, "just in case"? But such questions, though good, beg others. Those who work where personal data is handled should be bold about demanding accountability, and about the need for those who are classified for whatever purpose to be informed about and involved in the creation of categories.

Surveillance after September 11 places before us some momentous challenges. Above all is the challenge of how to confront a closed-off world of social exclusion and how to resist the rise of classificatory, clandestine power. During the Renaissance the idea took root that peace and prosperity could be engineered through science and technology, and this idea was bolstered by the European Enlightenment. Since then, the attempted engineering of security has become a key priority, spawning the myths mentioned above,[29] and contributing to the very difficulties we now face. The problem is that the Renaissance and Enlightenment encouraged an inversion of priorities. As I hinted at the start of this book, an appropriate ethic begins by hearing the voice of the Other. And social care starts with acceptance – not suspicion – of the Other. Such an ethic does not exist in a cultural vacuum, however. It grows like green shoots in the soil of shared visions of desired worlds. But such visions seem in short supply today, when history is downplayed by mass media and securing the present preoccupies politicians. Attempts to engineer peace and security have become the default position in a world of amplified fears and truncated hopes. This "fixing" mentality also tends to close off other options, as if they did not exist.

Jacques Ellul once noted, reflecting on the fate of ancient cities such as Babylon and Nineveh, that these cultures were closed, too, "protected against attacks from the outside, in a security built up in walls and machines."[30] Is there anything new under the sun? Yet against that, insists Ellul, is the vision of a city where doing justice and loving one's neighbor is put first. From that commitment to responsibility for the Other proceeds peace and prosperity, freedom and security, sought otherwise through false priorities. This is a city whose gates are never shut. It is a place of inclusion and trust. And its light finally banishes all that is now done in the dark.[31]

Notes

Introduction

1 See David Lyon, *The Electronic Eye: The Rise of Surveillance Society* (Cambridge: Polity Press, 1994); David Lyon and Elia Zureik (eds.), *Computers, Surveillance, and Privacy* (Minneapolis: University of Minnesota Press, 1996); David Lyon, *Surveillance Society: Monitoring Everyday Life* (Buckingham: Open University Press, 2001); David Lyon (ed.), *Surveillance as Social Sorting: Privacy, Risk, and Digital Discrimination* (London and New York: Routledge, 2002).

2 Quoted in Michael Richardson, "ASEAN to step up efforts with US in war on terror," *International Herald Tribune/Asahi Shimbun* (Tokyo edition), July 31, 2002: 2.

3 See e.g. David Garland, *The Culture of Control* (Chicago: University of Chicago Press, 2001).

4 See Ian Roxborough, "Globalization, unreason, and the dilemmas of American military strategy," *International Sociology*, 17 (3), 2002: 339–59.

5 Of course, technology derailed from its role as a servant of proper human purposes is likely to take on the appearance of savior. Cultures influenced by Christianity tread a knife-edge here. Once eyes are averted from a savior worthy of that name, then almost anything or anyone, it seems, will substitute.

6 I use the terms "care" and "control" in part to be consistent with my earlier work on surveillance. There has been a shift

away from "social control" as a category, however, and an
increasing interest in "governance." This is a welcome shift,
because "social control" can be read as a kind of reduction-
ism in which some persons or groups act on others. "Governance" acknowledges the participation of subjects in their
own surveillance, and their willingness, under some circumstances, to be surveilled. None the less, after September 11
certain agencies are "acting on others" in a more blatant
way, which justifies some continued use of the term
"control."

Chapter 1   Understanding Surveillance

1   Jacques Ellul, *The Technological Society* (New York: Knopf,
    1964), p. 100.
2   This may be seen on many web sites, e.g. <www.
    viisage.com>
3   <http://argument.independent.co.uk/leading_article/
    story.jsp> and <www.nytimes.com/2001/10/07/magazine/
    07SURVEILLANCE.html>
4   Philip Abrams, *Historical Sociology* (Shepton Mallett: Open
    Books, 1982), p. 191.
5   Ibid., p. 192.
6   Hannah Arendt, *The Origins of Totalitarianism* (New York:
    Harcourt, Brace, Jovanovich, 1951); Zygmunt Bauman,
    Modernity and the Holocaust (Cambridge: Polity, 1989).
7   T. Newman and S. Hayman, *Policing, Surveillance, and
    Social Control* (Cullompton UK: Willan Publishing, 2001).
8   Samuel Huntington's book, *The Clash of Civilizations and
    the Making of World Order* (New York: Simon and Schuster,
    1996), argues that the world is increasingly divided on
    "religious" civilization lines, a situation that will produce
    inevitable conflict. He works with what come down to racial
    stereotypes, suggesting that NATO be closed to countries
    that have historically been primarily Muslim or Orthodox.
    Moreover, the USA should police this exclusion to protect
    western civilization. This thesis is clearly predicated on the

superiority of certain civilizations and precludes the idea that western ones could be responsible for acts of terror. For a critique, see Mark Salter, *Barbarians and Civilizations in International Perspective* (London: Pluto Press, 2002).

9   I am indebted to Gerry Gill for this thought. For a treatment of contemporary "apocalypse," see Stephen F. Haller, *Apocalypse Soon? Wagering on Warnings of Global Catastrophe* (Montreal and Kingston: McGill-Queen's University Press, 2002).

10   Thomas Mathiesen, "The viewer society: Michel Foucault's 'panopticon' revisited," *Theoretical Criminology*, 1 (2), 1997: 215–34.

11   A relevant and readable background to the attacks may be found in Malise Ruthven, *A Fury for God: The Islamist Attack on America* (London and New York: Granta Books, 2002) and Dilip Hiro, *War without End: The Rise of Islamist Terrorism and Global Response* (London and New York: Routledge, 2002).

12   See further the discussion of the work of Jacques Lacan in Christian Metz, *The Imaginary Signifier: Psychoanalysis and the Cinema* (Bloomington IN: Indiana University Press, 1982). I am grateful to Victor Li for suggesting this text.

13   The USA's PATRIOT Act was followed quickly, in October 2001, by similar legislation in the UK, Canada, and in several other countries. Other countries had second thoughts on legislation as a result of September 11. In Germany, the draft of a new, more liberal immigration law was scrapped at the same time as laws regulating freedom of movement and requiring fingerprints in identity cards were tightened. See <www.nytimes.com/2001/10/01/international/europe/01GERM.html>

14   "New ID cards for landed immigrants," *Toronto Star*, October 11, 2001.

15   *Guardian*, October 30, 2001, <http://politics.guardian.co.uk/whitehall/story/0,,583304,00.html> Accessed October 30, 2001.

16   E. Higgs, "The rise of the information state: the development of central state surveillance of the citizen in England

1500–2000," *Journal of Historical Sociology*, 14 (2), 2001: 175–97.

17 E.g. Anthony Giddens, *The Nation State and Violence* (Cambridge: Polity, 1985); Michael Mann, *The Sources of Social Power*, vol. 1 (Cambridge: Cambridge University Press, 1986).

18 Higgs, "The Rise of the Information State."

19 Ibid., p. 180.

20 See Nicholas Abercrombie et al., *Sovereign Individuals of Capitalism* (London: Allen and Unwin, 1986).

21 See David Lyon, "British ID cards: the unpalatable cost of European membership?" *The Political Quarterly*, 62 (3), 1991: 377–85.

22 Higgs, "The Rise of the Information State," p. 190.

23 See Christopher Dandeker, *Surveillance Power and Modernity* (Cambridge: Polity, 1990).

24 F. Webster and K. Robins, *Information Technology: A Luddite Analysis* (Norwood, NJ: Ablex, 1986).

25 J. Beniger, *The Control Revolution: The Social and Economic Origins of the Information Society* (Cambridge, MA: Harvard University Press, 1986).

26 Gary T. Marx originated the concept of "categorical suspicion" in his *Undercover: Police Surveillance in America* (Berkeley: University of California Press, 1988) and its consumer parallel is discussed in D. Lyon, *Surveillance Society: Monitoring Everyday Life* (Buckingham: Open University Press, 2001).

27 D. Garland, *The Culture of Control: Crime and Social Order in Contemporary Society* (Chicago: University of Chicago Press, 2001).

28 A. Giddens, *The Consequences of Modernity* (Cambridge: Polity, 1990).

29 On this, see the insightful essay by Elia Zureik, "Theorizing surveillance: the case of the workplace," in David Lyon (ed.), *Surveillance as Social Sorting: Privacy, Risk, and Digital Discrimination* (London and New York: Routledge, 2002).

30 This is what Ulrich Beck calls "reflexive modernization."

See Ulrich Beck, Anthony Giddens, and Scott Lash, *Reflexive Modernization* (Cambridge: Polity, 1994).

31 This was noted early in the twentieth century by sociologists such as Georg Simmel.

32 See, e.g., Richard Sennett, *The Corrosion of Character* (New York: W. W. Norton, 1997).

33 See John Gilliom, *Overseers of the Poor: Surveillance, Resistance, and the Limits of Privacy* (Chicago: University of Chicago Press, 2001).

34 James B. Rule, *Private Lives and Public Surveillance* (London: Allen Lane, 1973).

35 See e.g. Mark Poster, "Databases as discourse," in David Lyon and Elia Zureik (eds.), *Computers, Surveillance, and Privacy* (Minneapolis: University of Minnesota Press, 1996).

36 This is persuasively argued by Anthony Giddens in *The Nation State and Violence* (Cambridge: Polity, 1985).

37 See, e.g., Roy Boyne, "Post-panopticism," *Economy and Society*, 29 (2), 2000: 285–307.

38 Clive Norris, "From personal to digital: the panopticon and the technological mediation of suspicion and control," in David Lyon (ed.), *Surveillance as Social Sorting: Privacy, Risk, and Digital Discrimination* (London and New York: Routledge, 2002).

39 Oscar Gandy, *The Panoptic Sort: A Political Economy of Personal Information* (Boulder CO: Westview, 1993); Richard Ericson and Kevin Haggerty, *Policing the Risk Society* (Toronto: University of Toronto Press, 1997).

40 <www.nytimes.com/2001/11/12/national/12STUD.html>

41 D. Lyon, "Surveillance after September 11," *Sociological Research Online*, 6 (3), 2001, <www.socresonline.org.uk/6/3/lyon>

42 K. Haggerty and R. Ericson, "The surveillant assemblage," *British Journal of Sociology*, 51 (4), 2000: 605–22.

43 Nikolas Rose, *Powers of Freedom* (Cambridge: Cambridge University Press, 1999), p. 234.

44 S. Crook, "Ordering risks," in D. Lupton (ed.), *Risk and Sociocultural Theory* (Cambridge: Cambridge University Press, 1995).

45 A longer survey appears in Lyon, *Surveillance Society*.
46 Quoted in <www.ssrc.org/sept11/essays/meyers.htm>
47 Lyon (ed.), *Surveillance as Social Sorting*.
48 Clive Norris and Gary Armstrong, *The Maximum Surveillance Society: The Rise of CCTV* (Oxford: Berg, 1999).
49 I experienced this, anecdotally, when an op-ed piece I wrote under the title "Whither surveillance after Bloody Tuesday?" was published in the newspaper as "What price in liberty will we pay for security?" *The Kingston Whig-Standard*, September 28, 2001.
50 This invites consideration of these themes from the viewpoint of Emile Durkheim, which focuses on social solidarities, rather than only Max Weber, for whom rationalization was the key.
51 See the work of Annette Baier, *Moral Prejudices: Essays on Ethics* (Cambridge, MA: Harvard University Press, 1994), pp. 1–17.

Chapter 2 Intensifying Surveillance

1 Margaret Drabble, interview in *The Queen's Quarterly*, 109 (3), 2002: 394.
2 See Paul Edwards's excellent account in *The Closed World: Computers and the Politics of Discourse in Cold War America* (Cambridge MA: MIT Press, 1996).
3 Peter Shields, "Beyond 'loss-of-control': Telecommunications, surveillance, drugs, and terrorism," *Journal of Policy, Regulation, and Strategy for Telecommunications and Media*, 4 (2), 2002: 9–15.
4 Gwynne Dyer, "The coming war," *Queen's Quarterly*, 109 (4), 2002: 498.
5 H. G. Wells, *The War in the Air* (New York, 1908); cited in Mike Davis, "The flames of New York," *New Left Review*, 12, Nov/Dec 2001: 52.
6 Thomas Marshall, *Citizenship and Social Class* (Cambridge: Cambridge University Press, 1950).
7 *The Globe and Mail* (Toronto) September 12, 2001: A1.

8   Slavoj Žižek, *Welcome to the Desert of the Real* (London and New York: Verso, 2002), p. 47.

9   See <http://cbc.ca/storyview/CBC/2002/09/12/pm_reax 020912>

10 Franz Neumann, *The Rule of Law: Political Theory and the Legal System in Modern Society* (Leamington Spa: Berg, 1986); quoted in Kanishka Jarasuriya, "9/11 and the new 'anti-politics' of 'security'," in Eric Hershberg and Kevin W. Moore (eds.), *Critical Views of September 11: Analyses from Around the World* (New York: The New Press).

11 Will Hutton, *The World We're In* (London: Little, Brown, 2002), p. 81. Eric Lichtblau, "Republicans want terror law made permanent," *New York Times*, April 9, 2003.

12 President George W. Bush signed the Homeland Security Act into law on November 25, 2002, and swore in the country's first Secretary of Homeland Security, Tom Ridge, on January 24, 2003.

13 See Ulrich Beck, *Risk Society: Towards a New Modernity* (London: Sage, 1992).

14 Kirk Makin, "Anti-terrorism action weak, ineffective, lawyers hear," *The Globe and Mail* (Toronto), August 13, 2002: A4.

15 James Risen, "US failed to act on warnings in '98 of a plane attack," *New York Times*, September 19, 2002, <www.nytimes.com/2002/09/19/politics/19INTE.html>

16 "Surveillance Powers," October 10, 2001, ACLU, <www.aclu.org/congress/patriot_chart.html>

17 Don Stuart, "The Anti-Terrorism Bill (Bill C-36): an unnecessary quick fix that permanently stains the Canadian criminal justice system," in *Terrorism, Law and Democracy* (Ottawa: Institute for the Administration of Justice, 2002), pp. 173–92.

18 Richard Falk, "Terrorist foundations of recent US foreign policy," in Alexander George (ed.), *Western State Terrorism* (Cambridge: Polity, 1991), pp. 109–10.

19 Thomas Mathiesen, "Expanding the concept of terrorism," in Phil Scraton (ed.), *Beyond September 11: An Anthology of Dissent* (London: Pluto Press, 2002), p. 87.

20   Ibid., p. 92.

21   Ford Fessenden and Michael Moss, "Going electronic, Denver reveals long-term surveillance," *New York Times*, 21 December, 2002, <www.nytimes.com/2002/12/21/technology/21PRIV.html/>

22

23   Ethnic categorization has some powerful effects, dividing invidiously between groups. See Richard Jenkins, "Rethinking ethnicity: identity, categorization, and power," *Ethnic and Racial Studies*, 17 (2), 1994: 197–219.

24   Frank Furedi, *The New Ideology of Imperialism* (London: Pluto, 1994), p. 116.

25   <www.statewatch.org>

26   <http://abcnews.go.com/sections/us/dailynews/uspatriot.020701.html>

27   Roy Gutman, Christopher Dickey, and Sami Yousafzai, "Guantanamo justice?" *Newsweek*, July 8, 2002: 40–1.

28   "Confusion over fate of Ottawa man deported from the US," November 20, 2002, <www.cbc.ca/news/indepth/targetterrorism/canadahomefront/>

29   Jacques Steinberg, "In sweeping campus canvasses, US checks on Mideast students," *New York Times*, November 12, 2001, <www.nytimes.com/2001/11/12/national/12STUD.html>

30   Lisa Guernsey, "What did you do before the war?" *New York Times*, November 22, 2002 <www.nytimes.com>

31   Tony Bunyan, "The war on freedom and democracy," 2002, available online from Statewatch <www.statewatch.org>

32   Naomi Klein, *Fences and Windows* (Toronto: Vintage Canada, 2002), p. 238.

33   *CAUT Bulletin*, 49 (7), 2002: A3. See also <www.campuswatch.org> where academic naming and shaming also occurs.

34   <www.nytimes.com/2003/02/21/international/ZIPROF.html>

35   Adam Liptak, Neil A. Lewis, and Benjamin Weiser, "After Sept 11, a legal battle over limits of civil liberty," *New York*

Times, August 4, 2002, <www.nytimes.com/2002/08/04/national/04CIVI.html>
36 <www.cnn.com/2002/US/09/13.alligator.alley>
37 Interestingly, this story, along with many others, has been picked up by weblogs or "bloggers" on the internet. In that space it offers alternative understandings of the "war on terrorism." See <www.warblogging.com/archives/00222.php/>
38 John Schwartz, "Some companies will release customer records on request" (2002) <www.nytimes.com/2002/12/18/technology/18RECO.html>
39 <www.citizencorps.com.gov/watch.html/>
40 See <www.nytimes.com/2002/12/30/international/asia/30AUST.html>
41 Gary T. Marx, *Undercover: Police Surveillance in America* (Berkeley: University of California Press, 1988), p. 207.
42 Ibid., p. 141.
43 Onora O'Neill, *A Question of Trust* (Cambridge: Cambridge University, 2002).

Chapter 3   Automating Surveillance

1 Langdon Winner, "Complexity, Trust, and Terror," *NetFuture*, 137, October 22, 2002
2 Zygmunt Bauman, *Liquid Modernity* (Cambridge: Polity Press, 2000).
3 C. Norris, J. Moran, and G. Armstrong, "Algorithmic surveillance: the future of automated visual surveillance," in C. Norris et al. (eds.), *Surveillance, Closed Circuit Television, and Social Control* (Aldershot UK: Ashgate, 1998).
4 See Manuel Castells, *The Rise of the Network Society* (Malden, MA: Blackwell, 2000).
5 Stanley Cohen, *Images of Social Control* (Oxford: Blackwell, 1985); Michael McCahill, *The Surveillance Web: The Rise of CCTV in an English City* (Cullompton UK: Willan, 2002).
6 This is discussed in David Lyon, *Surveillance Society: Monitoring Everyday Life* (Buckingham: Open University Press,

2001) and in David Lyon, "Everyday surveillance: personal data and social classifications," *Information, Communication, and Society*, 5 (2), 2002: 242–57.

7   See Paul Edwards, *The Closed World* (Cambridge, MA: MIT Press, 1996), pp. 64ff.

8   On changing prison security systems, for example, see Mona Lynch, "Selling 'security-ware'," *Punishment and Society*, 4 (3), 2002.

9   "Homeland security: high-tech starts kicking in," *Business Week Online*, September 16, 2002,

10 Lisa Gill, "Tech security companies thrive amid economic slump," *NewsFactor Network*, November 12, 2001, . An interesting and illuminating account of how Americans, including security businesses, responded to 9/11 is Steven Brill, After: *How America confronted the September 12 era* (New York: Simon and Schuster, 2003).

11 Patience Wait, "One year later: a special update," *Washington Post*, September 16, 2002, <www.washingtonpost.com/ ac2/wp-dyn/A63330–2002Sep10/>

12 Warren Leary, "Science-technology drive is urged to fight terror," *New York Times*, June 25, 2002,

13 Comparative share price information from <http://big charts.com/> September 2002.

14 Cynthia Webb, "One year later . . . ," *The Washington Post*, September 16, 2002.

15 Lisa Bowman, "CIA venture arm sees post 9/11 surge," *News.com*, 2002, <http://news.com.com/2102–1023– 861873.html/>

16 Robert Mullins, "9/11 climate providing new market," *Silicon Valley/San Jose Business Journal*, July 19, 2002, <http://sanjose.bizjournals.com/sanjose/stories/2002/07/22/ story7.html/>

17 Bowman, "CIA venture arm sees post 9/11 surge," n. 15.

18 This distinction between monitoring and identifying bene-

fited from discussion with Bart Simon of Concordia University.

19 Frank Rich, "Thanks for the heads-up," *New York Times*, op-ed, May 25, 2002.

20 At Schiphol, and at Heathrow, London, iris-scanning systems were planned well before 9/11. See, e.g. Catherine Greenman, "In the fast lane with your eye as passport," *New York Times*, August 2, 2001.

21 M. Simons, "Security on the brain, solutions in the eyes," *New York Times*, October 25, 2001, <www.nytimes.com/2001/10/25/international/europe/25AMST.html>

22 K. Pearsall, "This technology is eye-catching," *Computing Canada*, 24 (2), 1998: 11–12.

23 "Face scan to replace passport check," ABC News Online, January 29, 2003.

24 CBC, "Fingerprint scans part of new airport security," CBC news, October 11, 2001, <http://cbc.ca/cgi-bin/news 2001/10/11/airport_security.011011>

25 S. Costello, "Japanese researcher gums up biometrics scanners," *Infoworld*, May 16, 2002, <http://staging.infoworld.com/articles/hn/xml/02/05/16/020516hngumsxml?T>

26 <www.siliconvalley.com/cgi-bin/>

27 D. Francis, "Canadians master matching mug shots," *Financial Post*, October 19, 2000: C3.

28 G. T. Marx, "DNA 'fingerprints' may one day be our national ID card," *The Wall Street Journal*, April 20, 1998.

29 Reuters, "Microchips under the skin offer ID, raise questions," *The New York Times*, December 22, 2001, <www.nytimes.com/reuters/technology/tech-bizchips.html>

30 D. Lyon, "British identity cards: the unpalatable logic of European membership?" *The Political Quarterly*, 62 (3), 1991: 377–85; J. Agar, "Modern horrors: British identity and identity cards," in J. Caplan and J. Torpey (eds.), *Documenting Individual Identity: The Development of State Practices in the Modern World* (Princeton, NJ: Princeton University Press, 2001), pp. 101–20.

31 Felix Stalder, "Exploring political issues of electronic cash," *Canadian Journal of Communication*, 24 (2), 1999.

32   F. Stalder and D. Lyon, "ID cards and social classifica-
     tion," in D. Lyon (ed.), *Surveillance as Social Sorting:
     Privacy, Risk and Digital Discrimination* (London and New
     York: Routledge, 2002).

33   Kim Lunman, "Pre-1984 birth certificates could be ren-
     dered useless," *The Globe and Mail*, October 12, 2002:
     A12.

34   Ibid., p. A9.

35   Timothy Longman, "Identity cards, ethnic self-perception,
     and genocide in Rwanda," in John Torpey and Jane Caplan
     (eds.), *Documenting Individual Identity: The Development of
     State Practices in the Modern World* (Oxford and Princeton:
     Princeton University Press, 2001), pp. 345–58.

36   O. Burkeman, "Visa detainees allege beatings," *Guardian*,
     May 23, 2002.

37   L. Fernandez, "Oakland to be first UA airport to use face-
     recognition ID system" (2001) <www.siliconvalley.com/
     docs/hottopics/attack/image101801.htm>

38   P. R. Newswire, "Boston Logan airport chooses South
     Florida security company," October 31, 2001, <http://
     ir.shareholder.com/vsnx/
     ReleaseDetail.cfm?ReleaseID=63478>

39   C. Norris and G. Armstrong, *The Maximum Security
     Society: The Rise of CCTV* (London: Berg, 1999).

40   C. Wood, "The electronic eye view," *Mclean's*, November
     19, 2001: 94–7.

41   R. O'Harrow, "Matching faces with mug shots," *The Wash-
     ington Post*, August 1, 2001: A01; T. C. Greene, "Think-
     tank urges face-scanning of the masses," *The Register*,
     August 20, 2001, <www.theregister.co.uk/content/6/
     20966.html>

42   Francis, "Canadians master matching mug shots," *Finan-
     cial Post*, October 19, 2000: C3.

43   B. Schnier, "Biometrics in Airports" (2001) <www.
     extremetech.com/0,3428,a%253D15070,00.asp>

44   P. Agre, "Your Face is not a Bar Code" (2001) <http://
     dlis.gseis.ucla.edu/pagre/bar-code.html>

45   <www.nytimes.com/2001/09/18/national/18RULE.html>

46   <www.alcu.org/features/f11010a.html>
     <www.siliconvalley.com/docs/hottopics/attack/
     image101801.htm> <http://sg.news.yahoo.com/011102/12/
     lne83.html>

47   D. Lyon, "Surveillance after September 11," *Sociological
     Research Online*, 6 (3), 2001, <www.socresonline.org.uk/6/
     3/lyon>

48   See William Bogard, *The Simulation of Surveillance: Hyper-
     control in Telematic Societies* (New York: Cambridge Univer-
     sity Press, 1996); Lyon, *Surveillance Society*, pp. 116–20.

49   David Lyon, *The Electronic Eye: The Rise of Surveillance
     Society* (Cambridge: Polity Press, 1994), pp. 211–17.

50   One can, of course, expand the definition of privacy to
     encompass the emerging situation, but at some point a new
     vocabulary will have to be created. Philip Agre, for
     instance, suggests how much broader the definition will
     have to be: "privacy is not just a matter of control over
     data; it also pertains to the regimentation of diverse aspects
     of everyday life through the socio-technical mechanisms by
     which data are produced." From the introduction to Philip
     Agre and Marc Rotenberg (eds.), *Technology and Privacy:
     The New Landscape* (Cambridge: MIT Press, 1997), p. 8.

51   Mike Davis, "The flames of New York," *New Left Review*,
     12, Nov/Dec, 2001: 50.

52   Desmond Butler and Don Van Natta, "Qaeda informant
     helps trace group's trail," <www.nytimes.com/2003/02/17/
     international/Europe/17QAED.html>

53   See also, e.g., Lloyd Axworthy's "human security"
     approach. This Canadian perspective draws attention to
     a broader range of issues than is often associated with
     "security." See, e.g., <www.wagingpeace.org/articles/01/
     09/010917axworthy.htm>

54   J. Rosen, "Silicon Valley's spy game," *The New York Times*,
     April 14, 2002, <www.nytimes.com/2002/04/14/magazine/
     14TECHNO.html>

55   Elaine Draper, "Drug-testing in the workplace: the allure
     of management technologies," *International Journal of Soci-
     ology and Social Policy*, 18 (5/6), 1998: 62–103.

56 David Noble, *The Religion of Technology: The Divinity of Man and the Spirit of Invention* (New York: Penguin, 1996).
57 Quoted in John Armitage, "From modernism to hypermodernism and beyond," *Theory, Culture, and Society*, 16 (5), 1999: 25–55.
58 "State of emergency" ideas relating to 9/11 are discussed in a special issue of *Theory, Culture, and Society*, 19 (4), 2002.
59 Faith in new technologies is even shared, it seems, by groups such as the American Civil Liberties Union, which warn that the technologies are not *yet* good enough to serve the purposes claimed for them.
60 Knowledge of Ellul's work is often limited only to the allegedly deterministic *The Technological Society* (New York: Vintage, 1964). But he saw his sociological work as integrated with his more theological writings that are anything but deterministic. It is misleading to see his most famous work out of the context of the whole corpus.
61 Bruce Schneier *Secrets and Lies: Digital Security in a Networked World* (New York: Wiley, 2000). See also the interview with Schneier in Charles C. Mann, "Homeland Insecurity," *The Atlantic Monthly*, September 2002, <www.theatlantic.com/09/2002/mann.html>

Chapter 4   Integrating Surveillance

1 Defense Advanced Research Projects Agency <www.darpa.mil/iao/index.htm/>
2 American House and Senate negotiators agreed with the Senate's findings that the system should not be approved without consulting with Congress. See Adam Clymer, "Conferees in Congress bar using Pentagon project on Americans," *New York Times*, February 12, 2003. DARPA officials have tried to reassure Congress that TIA can be limited; see Adam Clymer, "Pentagon surveillance plan is described as less invasive," *New York Times*, May 7, 2003.

3 EPIC briefing, November 2002, <www.epic.org/events/tia_briefing/>

4 This and other quotations are from the TIA official web site <www.darpa.mil/iao/TIASystems.htm>

5 Anthony Deanna and Oscar Gandy, "All that glitters is not gold: digging beneath the surface of data mining," *Journal of Business Ethics*, 40, 2002: 373–86.

6 John Markoff, "Study seeks technology safeguards for privacy," *New York Times*, December 19, 2002, <www.nytimes.com/2002/12/19/national/19COMP.html>

7 David Johnston, "Administration begins to rewrite decades old spying restrictions," *New York Times*, November 30, 2002, <www.nytimes.com/2002/11/30/national/30INTE.html>

8 See, e.g., David Lyon, "Surveillance in cyberspace: the Internet, personal data, and social control," *The Queen's Quarterly*, 109 (3), 2002: 345–56.

9 The significance of this is discussed in Lawrence Lessig, *Code and Other Laws of Cyberspace* (New York: Basic Books, 1999).

10 Ibid., p. 151.

11 Oscar Gandy, *The Panoptic Sort: A Political Economy of Personal Information* (Boulder, CO: Westview, 1993).

12 Clive Norris and Gary Armstrong, *The Maximum Surveillance Society: The Rise of CCTV* (London: Berg, 1999).

13 Stephen Graham and David Wood, "Digitising surveillance: categorisation, space, inequality," *Critical Social Policy*, 26 (2), 2003.

14 Janet Gilboy, "Deciding who gets in: decision-making by immigration inspectors," *Law and Society Review*, 25 (3), 1991: 573.

15 I am indebted to Paula Abood for this expression.

16 See, e.g., <www.cnn.com/2001/TRAVEL/NEWS/10/03/rec.airlines.profiling/>

17 Philip Shenon and David Johnston, "Seeking terrorist plots, FBI is tracking hundreds of Muslims," *The New York Times*, October 6, 2002, <www.nytimes.com/2002/10/06/national/06SLEE.html/>

18   See Michael Meehan, "Iris scans take off at airports,"
     Computer World, July 17, 2000; Ricard Alfonso-Zaldivar,
     "'Trusted' air travelers would minimize wait," *Los Angeles
     Times*, February 12, 2002.
19   David Garland, *The Culture of Control: Crime and Social
     Order in Contemporary Society* (Chicago: University of Chi-
     cago Press, 2001), pp. 182–90.
20   Ibid., p. 183.
21   Ibid., p. 184.
22   Paul Virilio, *The Vision Machine* (Bloomington: Indiana
     University Press, 1994).
23   Gilles Deleuze, "Postscript on the societies of control,"
     October, 59, 1992: 3–7.
24   E.g. Richard Jones, "Digital rule: punishment, control, and
     technology," *Punishment and Society*, 2 (1), 2000: 5–22.
25   On "disappearing bodies," see David Lyon, *Surveillance
     Society: Monitoring Everyday Life* (Buckingham: Open Uni-
     versity Press, 2001).
26   Garland, *The Culture of Control*, p. 205.
27   See, e.g., Nikolas Rose, *Powers of Freedom* (Cambridge:
     Cambridge University Press, 1999).
28   Judith Miller, "Report calls for plan of sharing data to
     prevent terror," *New York Times*, October 7, 2002,
     <www.nytimes.com/2002/10/07/national/07HOME.html>
29   Eric Lichtblau, "FBI and CIA set for major consolidation
     in counter-terror," <www.nytimes.com/2003/02/15/politics/
     15THRE.html>
30   See Steve Graham and Simon Marvin, *Splintering Urban-
     ism: Networked Infrastructures, Technological Mobilities, and
     the Urban Condition* (London: Routledge, 2001).

Chapter 5   Globalizing Surveillance

1   "New terror task force," <www.cbsnews.com/stories/2001/
    05/08/national/main290081.shtml>
2   Didier Bigo, "Security and immigration: towards a critique

of the governmentality of unease," *Alternatives*, 27, 2002: 63–92.

3   For useful introductory discussions of the meanings of globalization, see, e.g., David Held and Anthony McGrew, *Globalization/Anti-Globalization* (Cambridge: Polity, 2002), and Malcolm Waters, *Globalization* (London and New York: Routledge, 1995).

4   Zygmunt Bauman characterizes this distinction as between "tourists" and "vagabonds." Tourists travel where they wish, because they want to and because they find certain places attractive. Vagabonds travel because they have to, because they find where they are is unbearably inhospitable. See *Globalization: The Human Consequences* (New York: New York University Press, 1998), pp. 77–102.

5   Benjamin Barber, *Jihad versus McWorld* (New York: Times Books, 1995).

6   See David Lyon, "Fundamentalisms: Paradoxical products of postmodernity," in Chris Partridge (ed.), *Fundamentalisms* (Carlisle, UK: Paternoster, 2001).

7   John Urry, "The global complexities of September 11," *Theory, Culture and Society*, 19 (4), 2002: 57–69

8   Naomi Klein observes that protesters against the World Trade Organization and its cognates experience globalization as lived reality, and even celebrate it. It is the effects of certain kinds of economic, political, and cultural globalization that are in question, not globalization itself. See *Fences and Windows: Dispatches from the Front Lines of the Globalization Debate* (Toronto: Vintage Canada, 2002), p. xv.

9   This threefold scheme owes much to David Held and Anthony McGrew (eds.), *Global Transformations: Politics, Economics, and Culture* (Cambridge: Polity Press, 2000).

10 Manuel Castells, *The Rise of the Network Society* (Malden, MA: Blackwell, 2000).

11 Bauman, *Globalization*.

12 Barber, *Jihad vs McWorld*.

13 Although he does not argue this, the idea took root when I read the pamphlet by Peter Heslam, *Globalization: Unravelling the New Capitalism* (Cambridge: Grove Books, 2002).

14   Ibid., p. 20.
15   Kanishka Jayasuriya, "9/11 and the new 'anti-politics' of 'security'" (2002) <www.ssrc.org/sept11/essays/jayasuriya. htm/>
16   Duncan Campbell and Steven Connor, *On the Record: Computers, Surveillance, and Privacy* (London: Michael Joseph, 1986); Nicky Hager, *Secret Power: New Zealand's Role in the International Spy Network* (Nelson, NZ: Craig Potton Publishing, 1996).
17   Steve Wright, *An Appraisal of Technologies of Political Control* (European Parliament, Scientific and Technological Options Assessment, January 1998).
18   Thomas Mathiesen, *On Globalization of Control: Towards an Integrated Surveillance System in Europe* (London: Statewatch, 1999), p. 2.
19   Ibid., p. 3.
20   Kevin Haggerty and Richard Ericson, "The militarization of policing in the information age," *Journal of Political and Military Sociology*, 27, 1999: 233–45.
21   David Lyon, *The Electronic Eye* (Cambridge: Polity, 1994), pp. 150–3.
22   Bien Perez, "State agencies turn to analytics to fight terrorists," *South China Morning Post*, October 4, 2001, <http:// technology.scmp.com/cgi-bin/gx.cgi/ AppLogic+FTContentServer?pagename=S>
23   Duncan Campbell, "How the plotters slipped US net," *The Guardian Online*, September 27, 2001: 1–2.
24   Ron Deibert and Janice Stein, "Hacking networks of terror," in *International Organization Dialogue* (Cambridge: Cambridge University Press, 2002), p. 16.
25   CNN, "Net effect: anti-terror eavesdropping," (2002) <http://www.cnn.com/2002/TECH/internet/05/27/terror. surveillance.ap/index.html>
26   S. A. Mathiesen, "The net's eyes are watching," *Guardian*, November 15, 2001, <www.guardian.co.uk/ 0,3858,4298,894,00.html>
27   Associated Press, "Internet takes on police role worldwide," *South China Morning Post*, November 23, 2001,

<http://technology.scmp.com/cgi-bin/gx-cgi/AppLogic+
FTContentServer?pagename=S . . . _23/11/01>

28   S. Millar, "Police get sweeping access to net data,"
     Guardian, November 7, 2001, <www.guardian.co.uk/
     0,3058,4293489,00.html>
29   A. L. Pennenberg, "Surveillance Society," *Wired*, Decem-
     ber 2001: 157–60.
30   J. Urry, *Sociology Beyond Societies: Mobilities for the Twenty-
     First Century* (London: Routledge, 2000), p. 50.
31   M. Gottdiener, *Life in the Air: Surviving the New Culture of
     Air Travel* (Lanham MD: Rowman and Littlefield, 2001),
     p. 1.
32   Allan Thompson, "Privacy under stack: watchdog," *Toronto
     Star*, November 24, 2002: A1.
33   Mark Salter, "Passports, mobility, and security: how smart
     can the border be?" *International Studies Perspectives*
     (forthcoming).
34   See, e.g., Oscar Gandy, *The Panoptic Sort: A Political Econ-
     omy of Personal Information* (Boulder: Westview, 1993)
35   See David Lyon, *The Electronic Eye: The Rise of Surveillance
     Society* (Cambridge: Polity, 1994), p. 156.
36   This was true of several systems before 9/11, and similar
     processes are still in place now. However, these procedures
     are under review and are subject to change in the post-9/11
     situation.
37   Colin J. Bennett, "What happens when you buy an airline
     ticket? Surveillance, globalization, and the regulation of
     international communications networks," paper presented
     at the Canadian Political Science Association, June 6,
     1999.
38   Ibid., p. 6.
39   See Mark Salter, *Rights of Passage* (Boulder, CO: Lynne
     Rienner, 2003).
40   M. Gladwell, "Safety in the skies: how far can airline
     security go?" *The New Yorker*, October 1, 2001, <www.
     newyorker.com/fact.content/?011001fa_FACT#top>
41   See Gladwell, "Safety in the skies."
42   R. O'Harrow, "Intricate screening of fliers in works," *The

Washington Post, February 1, 2002: A01 <http://www.washingtonpost.com/ac2/wp-dyn/A5185-2002Jan31>

43   See Gary T. Marx, *Undercover: Police Surveillance in America* (Berkeley: University of California Press, 1988) and D. Lyon, *The Electronic Eye: The Rise of Surveillance Society* (Cambridge: Polity, 1994).

44   Geoffrey Bowker and Susan Leigh Star, *Sorting Things Out: Classification and its Consequences* (Cambridge, MA: MIT Press, 1999).

45   Richard Ericson and Kevin Haggerty, *Policing the Risk Society* (Toronto: University of Toronto Press, 1997).

46   William Bogard, *The Simulation of Surveillance* (New York: Cambridge University Press, 1996).

47   E. Borin, "Private Information Becoming Plane Truth," *Wired*, September 16, 2002, <www.wired.com/news/print/0,1294,55037,00.html>

48   M. Wald, "Boston Airport to Install Scanners," *New York Times*, September 23, 2002, <www.nytimes.com/2002/09/23/technology/23BOST.html>

49   Clive Norris, "From the personal to the digital," in David Lyon, (ed.), *Surveillance as Social Sorting* (London and New York: Routledge, 2002).

50   Stephen Graham and David Wood, "Digitizing surveillance: categorisation, space, inequality," *Critical Social Policy*, 26 (2), 2003.

51   See Gladwell, "Safety in the skies." See note xxii.

52   Michael Ignatieff, "The burden," *New York Times Magazine*, January 5, 2003.

53   Michael Richardson, "ASEAN to step up efforts with US in war on terror," *International Herald Tribune* with *Asahi Shimbun*, July 31, 2002: 2.

54   Document circulated by the "Civil Society Concerned about Globalizing Law Enforcement," obtained from Ogura Toshimaru, Toyama University, Japan.

55   James Norman, "Snoop systems scrutinized," *The Australian*, July 23, 2002: 4.

56   See Colin Bennett, *Regulating Privacy* (Ithaca: Cornell University Press, 1992) and David Flaherty, *Protecting Privacy*

in Surveillance Societies (Chapel Hill: University of North Carolina Press, 1989).

57 See Priscilla Regan, "The globalization of privacy: implications of recent changes in Europe," *The American Journal of Economics and Sociology*, 52 (3), 1993: 257–74.

58 Naomi Klein, *Fences and Windows: Dispatches from the Front Lines of the Globalization Debate* (Toronto: Vintage Canada, 2002).

59 Saskia Sassen, "Towards a sociology of information technology," *Current Sociology*, 50 (3), 2002.

Chapter 6   Resisting Surveillance

1 Ursula Franklin, Science for Peace Forum, December 9, 2001, <http://scienceforpeace.sa.utoronto.ca/Special_Activities/Franklin_Page.html/>

2 David Garland, *The Culture of Control* (University of Chicago Press, 2001).

3 Onora O'Neill, *A Question of Trust* (Cambridge: Cambridge University Press, 2002), ch. 2.

4 Kevin Haggerty and Richard Ericson, "The surveillant assemblage," *British Journal of Sociology*, 54 (1), 2000.

5 Pierre Bourdieu, *Distinction: A Social Critique of the Judgment of Taste* (London and New York: Routledge, 1986), pp. 480–1. Thanks to Craig Calhoun for reminding me of this.

6 This distinction, plus one other, "exclusion as assimilation," comes from Miroslav Volf, *Exclusion and Embrace: A Theological Exploration of Identity, Otherness, and Reconciliation* (Nashville: Abingdon, 1996), p. 75.

7 E.g. William Safire, "You are a suspect," *New York Times*, November 14, 2002 <www.nytimes.com/2002/11/14/opinion/14SAFI.html/> Good points are made but they do not go nearly far enough.

8 Anthony Giddens, *The Nation-State and Violence*; vol 2: *A Contemporary Critique of Historical Materialism* (Cambridge: Polity Press, 1985).

9   John Gilliom, *Overseers of the Poor* (Chicago: University of Chicago Press, 2001).

10   William Diffie and Susan Landau, *Privacy on the Line: The Politics of Wiretapping and Encryption* (Cambridge, MA: MIT Press, 1998).

11   Michael J. Weiss, *The Clustering of America* (New York: Harper and Row, 1988).

12   Ulrich Beck, "The terrorist threat: world risk society revisited," *Theory, Culture, and Society*, 19 (4), 2002.

13   See the 2002 report, "Bigger monster, weaker chains," at <www.aclu.org/privacy/privacylist.cfm?c=39>

14   "Japan in uproar as 'Big Brother' computer file kicks in," <www.nytimes.com/2002/08/06/international/asia/06JAPA.html>

15   Lawrence Lessig, *Code and Other Laws of Cyberspace* (New York: Basic Books, 1999).

16   Lucy Suchman, "Do categories have politics?" *Computer Supported Cooperative Work*, 2 (1), 1994: 177–90.

17   Ian Barns, "Technological citizenship," in Alan Petersen, Ian Barns, Janice Dudley, and Patricia Harris, *Post-Structuralism, Citizenship, and Social Policy* (London: Routledge, 1999).

18   Langdon Winner, "Complexity, trust, and terror," *NetFuture*, 137, October 22, 2002,

19   See Langdon Winner, "Technologies as forms of life," in his *The Whale and the Reactor: A Search for Limits in an Age of High Technology* (Chicago: University of Chicago Press, 1986) and Ian Barns, "The renewal of civic virtue and the difference technology makes," unpublished paper, Sustainable Technology Policy Unit, Murdoch University, Perth, Australia, 2001.

20   David Noble, *The Religion of Technology: The Divinity of Man and the Spirit of Invention* (London: Penguin, 1997).

21   James W. Carey and James J. Quirk, "The mythos of the electronic revolution," *American Scholar*, 39 (1), 1970: 219–41, and 39 (2), 1970: 395–424.

22   See Richard Jenkins, "Categorization: identity, social pro-

cess, and epistemology," *Current Sociology*, 48 (3), 2000: 7–25. He argues that rather than focusing on the fashionable "reflexive self-identity," sociology ought to be far more concerned with categorization.

23 Sissela Bok, *Secrets: On the Ethics of Concealment and Revelation* (Oxford: Oxford University Press, 1982), p. 106.

24 See Kanishka Jayasuriya, "9/11 and the new 'anti-politics' of 'security'," (2002) <www.ssrc.org/sept11/essays/jayasuriya.htm/>

25 Ibid.

26 Hannah Arendt, *The Origins of Totalitarianism* (New York: Harcourt, Brace, Jovanovich, 1951).

27 One could argue, of course, that the US administration has supplied and supported terrorist states elsewhere, and is thus at least complicit in state terrorism. See, e.g. John Pilger, *The New Rulers of the World* (London: Verso, 2002).

28 Craig Calhoun, "Plurality, promises, and public spaces," in Craig Calhoun and John McGowan (eds.), *Hannah Arendt and the Meaning of Politics* (Minneapolis: University of Minnesota Press, 1997), p. 236.

29 Bob Goudzewaard, *Idols of our Time* (Downers Grove: Inter-Varsity Press, 1984), p. 66.

30 Jacques Ellul, *The Meaning of the City* (Grand Rapids: Eerdmans, 1970), p. 76.

31 Ibid., pp. 192–3.

Index